The NUMERICAL STRUCTURE of the TORAH,
A Logistical Primer

The NUMERICAL STRUCTURE of the TORAH,
A Logistical Primer

Phillip E. Stiefel Sr.

We are learning about the Torah solely from its context.

MILL CITY PRESS

Mill City Press, Inc.
2301 Lucien Way #415
Maitland, FL 32751
407.339.4217
www.millcitypress.net

Unless otherwise noted, the Torah's verses are from the Bible Scholar Software, used by permission.

Cover by Graphics by the author.

The Numerical Structure of The Torah, A Logistical Primer (First edition) by Phillip E. Stiefel

Paperback ISBN-13: 978-1-66280-862-3
Ebook ISBN-13: 978-1-66280-863-0

Dedication

Plymouth Colony Established 1620 CE

This work is dedicated to my ancestral pilgrim grandparents: John Tilley and Joan Hurst Rogers, John and Elizabeth (Tilley) Howland. Four hundred years ago, my ancestors traversed a vast and terrifying sea in search of a place where they could live in peace and plumb the depths of their scriptures. My ancestral grandfather, John Howland, was cast into the torrid depth of the Atlantic, and by the grace of the Creator, he survived. It is recorded that upon the pilgrims' first landing; those brave voyagers prayed in the Hebrew language.

Unlike my pilgrim ancestors, who plumbed the depths of many texts with a multitude of teachers in search of their fathers' truths, I have returned to the foundation of their messianic faith, the Torah, and the teachings of Moses.

With Moses as my guide, I have endeavored to understand my Father's words, as a *"maskil,"* a man of understanding, who is seeking the Creator (Ps. 14:2).

Epigraph

Jeremiah 9:22-23
Thus says the Lord,
Let not the wise man glory in his wisdom,
nor let the mighty man glory in his might,
let not the rich man glory in his riches:

But let him who glories glory in this,
that he understands and knows me,
that I am the Lord who exercises loving kindness,
justice, and righteousness, in the earth;
for in these things I delight, says the Lord:
Bible Scholar Text

Table of Contents

Preface

I did not set out to search for an embedded numerical structure, nor was I searching for any profound revelations. I saw a numerical connection in the "Shema" passage of the Torah, and I followed the path of the infinite numerical connections, the likes of which were and remain unimaginable. This book is the result of making numerous numerical connections, which are only remotely related to the study of gematria or numerology. The only reliable language connection that I possessed at the start was that I had a good understanding of reading comprehension skills, which I acquired from being a professional teacher for seven years.

The Hebrew word *echad*, "one," as found in the "Shema" passage (Deut. 6:4), has an ordinal numerical value of thirteen. In Hebrew, the consonants also function as numerals. Thus, there is a divine numerical connection between "one" and "thirteen," so in a manner of playful study, I looked to see if there are any exciting connections to be made with the number thirteen.

Since I was nine years old, I always knew inside of myself that God was my Father. I was not born into a religious family, and I did not attend any church. How I came to know the Creator as my Father, I cannot explain to this day. Why, one might ask, is that significant to the writing of this book? Well, the Hebrew word *avi* means "my father," and it has an ordinal value of thirteen. The Creator, my Father, thirteen, and one are all numerically connected. When I was twenty-seven years old, and in desperate straits, I turned to my Father and cried to him for miraculous intervention. He heard my plea, He came immediately to my assistance, and that has been our continuous relationship for over forty-five years.

It was made clear to me that I must understand His teachings in the language that it was spoken, and that has been a difficult task for me. I studied Latin in high school, Biblical Greek and Modern Hebrew in college, as well as a few courses in Biblical Hebrew on my own; however, I knew that I had not achieved the skills which I was directed to learn. However, the Shema passage and thirteen became the gateway to my Father's Hebrew. This book presents what I lovingly call *my Father's Hebrew*, which I was instructed to learn over forty-five years ago. I am humbled that I could have been given such a gift. This course of study is an invitation to an intimate conversation with our Father, the Creator. Any person can enter this conversation with minimal linguistic training.

There is one limiting factor; one must seek Him with all his intellect, with all his being, and with all his strength. One must find the Creator's perspective aside from man's perspective, to know Him as He desires to be known.

Don't stumble over the hard questions in life, come to your Father, and expect an answer. Most scholars, theologians, and philosophers have knowledge of God, but the Torah teaches about a loving Father who communicates with His children. What kind of decent father would ignore his children's voices? I have asked the hard questions throughout my life; I always expect answers. Our Father speaks; come, hear and learn of my Father's Hebrew.

Acknowledgments

My Father, My Master, and My God

Herein is what I lovingly call my Father's Hebrew. In the early winter of 1975, I received an inkling of something unique that I would be privileged to share. The journey from inkling to reality encompassed over forty years. I have been blessed like Caleb and Joshua to have stood the test of time and behold the promise in this life. I would not let go of him, and he would not let go of me. What is expressed herein is not a result of any academic credentials or linguistic talents on my part; it is merely a loving Father teaching His son the marvelous truths of His Torah in a uniquely powerful manner. I never could envision myself in a heaven. I could not imagine a stained soul such as myself living in the presence of a Holy God. Therefore, I put little stock in a place called heaven. My Father's Hebrew brought the above to my earthly soul, here and now, on earth. As far as death, the afterlife, or maybe even a place called heaven, they are hardly a concern, for as my Father said long ago concerning Adam, "It is not good for man to be alone" (Gen. 2:18). Therefore, I shall never be alone. Blessed be my Father, my Master, and my God.

My Wife Patricia

I have been married to my loving wife for over forty years. Our marriage was arranged by our Father, we both have continuously marveled over the wonder of it. In times of stress and joyfulness, it has carried us. It takes a special woman to wander hand in hand through the wilderness for forty years, and she has excelled at sharing the load, while never grumbling along the way. We have made it together, and her physical and spiritual labors are welled up in this text along with mine. I could not have fulfilled my Father's plan without this special woman.

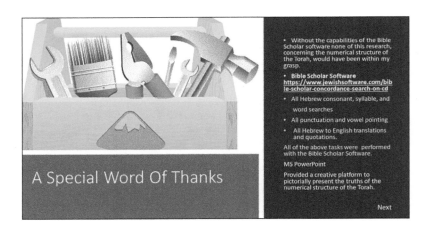

Introduction

The Purpose of This Book Is...

I ndeed, the purpose is of divine design, because I did not set out to search for a numerical structure, nor was I searching for any profound revelations. I saw a numerical connection in the "Shema" passage.

> *Devarim 6:4. Hear, O Israel; The Lord our God is one Lord:*

This book is simply the result of making numerous numerical connections, which are only remotely related to the study of gematria or numerology. The only reliable language connection that I possessed from the start was that I had a good understanding of reading comprehension skills, which I acquired from being a professional teacher for seven years.

The Hebrew word *echad*, "one," has an ordinal numerical value of thirteen. In Hebrew, the consonants also function as numerals, both ordinally and linguistically. Thus, there is a divine numerical connection between "one" and "thirteen," so in a manner of playful study, I looked to see if there are any exciting connections to be made with the number thirteen. Most significantly, the Hebrew word *avi*, "my Father," also has an ordinal value of thirteen. After almost five years of intense study of the Torah text, from the numerical perspective, the result is what I lovingly refer to as "my Father's Hebrew."

The numerical precepts which I have learned may turn the tables, and some of the traditional roles of study are about to be expanded. Perhaps, what is most exciting is that with the mastery of a few necessary skills and a desire to seek the Creator and not merely an eloquence of His Torah, the sincere seeker may now possess a personal tool of empowerment.

There are no outside sources employed in the research. The only source is the Torah. This book is all about context; therefore, all interpretations must be developed from within that context. Neither this book nor this author considers the Torah text to be the product of multiple authors. The Torah is not an inspired text; it is a divine text. When one is exposed to the numerical complexity of the text of the Torah, such liberal arguments may find themselves resting upon unstable ground. Not for one minute do I assume that everyone accepts the Torah as such, but for those whose hearts are turned toward the Creator, they shall find great amazement in this marvelous Torah.

The Goal of This Book Is...

The goal of this effort is that the reader may personally experience the Creator's teachings concerning the multiple contexts in which the Creator presented them and that we, as seekers, might better be able to know Him, as He desires to be known.

The Context of This Book Is...

The context of this book is focused on the numerical structure of the Torah, which is the embedded structural context of the Torah. No outside sources are employed to unveil this divine structure; therefore, the only coercive implications on the part of the author shall be to encourage the reader to discover the truths found in the Torah. No one shall be urged to convert to any organized religious group; it is the Creator that is the focus of this book.

Primarily, the context of this book is concerned with the numerical aspect of the Torah. There are two aspects of the Torah: first, the numerical structure, and second, the linguistic foliage. Before this author's efforts, the numerical structure has had little investigation or discussion, at least as far I know. Structure always precedes the outer embellishments; therefore, the analysis of the numerical structure is brought to the forefront. Indeed, the embellishments are indispensable, but first things should come first.

About the Organization of This Book...

A substantial effort has been put forth to present this discussion in a logical order so that the reader can understand the process from the ground up and have a model from which to proceed on his own. The reader is deliberately introduced first to the critical terminology as part of a pre-reading strategy. Likewise, the material is accompanied by visual illustrations to help varied learning styles. A concentrated effort has been made to address the "why" questions and demonstrate the benefits of the structure.

About the Scope of This Book...

This book does not address all the evidence and dynamics of the numerical structure of the Torah. I have been intensely studying this numerical structure for almost five years, and I find new significances and applications daily. *The numerical structure of the Torah* is a primer which only defines and demonstrates this phenomenon of light, which has burst upon the world of Torah investigation. This book is a how-to primer, which awaits the readers to become researchers and employ the strategy in all aspects of Torah research.

Invitation

Pre-Reading Terminology

Pre-Reading

When a reader engages with a book, whether it be a casual or deliberate action, he immediately embraces the book on his terms and within the limits of his prior knowledge. As the reader progresses through the book, he is forced to compare his sense of the book's terminology with the author's understanding. This learning process can, at least initially, impede the reader's comprehension of the author's message. Therefore, this pre-reading terminology has been introduced before the body of the composition, rather than in a later glossary.

Terminology

There is an adage that appropriately applies here, "coming to terms with a matter," or more precisely, "defining the terms of a matter." In the next picture are some of the critical terms related to the discussion or the

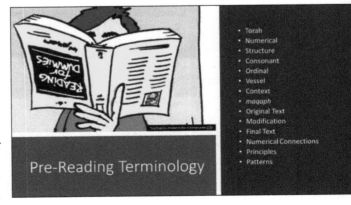

numerical structure of the Torah, as presented in this book. Although this is not a complete list of essential words, it is a list of the critical terms that are pertinent to the matter at hand.

Every subject of a critical investigation has its unique terminology. Understanding the author's vocabulary is paramount to understanding the context of the discussion. Context is both a friend and a foe of conversation. Misunderstanding a term within its context can lead to faulty conclusions, disagreement, and many other unfortunate outcomes.

The book, *The Numerical Structure of the Torah*, has its unique terminology, much like the avian illustration below.

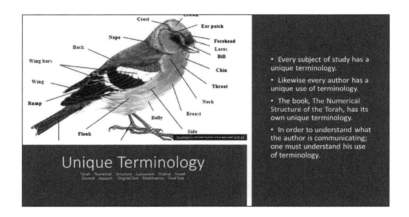

The Torah

Torah is a Hebrew word that can have a multitude of meanings, particularly among Jewish people. The Hebrew word *Torah* (תּוֹרָה) is first found in the Hebrew Bible in *Shemot* (Exod. 12:49) and is related to the divine rules of behavior.

"One law Torah (תּוֹרָה) *shall be for him who is native born, and for the stranger who sojourns among you"*:

The Hebrew word Torah is related to teaching and instruction. The divine instructions given to man are recorded in the first five books of the Hebrew Bible. Therefore, these first five books have come to be called the Torah.

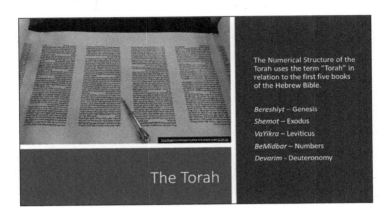

The Numerical Structure of the Torah uses the term "Torah" in relation to the first five books of the Hebrew Bible.

Bereshiyt – Genesis
Shemot – Exodus
VaYikra – Leviticus
BeMidbar – Numbers
Devarim - Deuteronomy

The Torah

However, in a more liberal sense, the word Torah has been linked to any other text or teaching that stems from the divine instructions contained in the first five books of the Hebrew Bible. The Torah is traditionally written on a scroll as depicted in the picture above; when it is written in a book format, it is referred to as the Chumash. Therefore, the terms Torah and Chumash are similar when it comes to their relationship to the first five books of the Hebrew Bible, and it is in this sense that the terms *Torah* and *Chumash* are used concerning the numerical structure. This book could just as well have been called The Numerical Structure of The Chumash.

Numerical

Perhaps one of the most challenging concepts that one incurs when contemplating the numerical structure of the Torah is that the structure must precede the composition of the textual characters. A builder does not install the windows, doors, roofing, and siding before fabricating the structural framework.

The structure must precede the embellishments, and if that structure is numerical, then the numerical aspect precedes the linguistical element. Imagine that the numerical design preceded the alphabetic composition. The designer began numerically, and he related the numerical aspect with the alphabetic feature. It might surprise you that the Torah begins with the numeral "2," which is also the consonant "*beit.*"

The Hebrew alphabet also uses the consonants as numerals. Thus, the first ten consonants are related to the numbers one through ten; however, from the eleventh letter on, the consonants do not refer consecutively to the numbers eleven and following. The numerical structure of the Torah does not use this literary system of numerical relationships; it views each consonant as an ordinal number.

Given all the above, it is imperative to understand that the term *numerical* can embrace a multitude of relationships involving the written text. Consider the astronomers who probe the vastness of the universe using both numbers and words and imagine the futility of investigating the mysteries of space without the aid of numbers.

Structure

Whatever one's rational concept of the meaning of *structure* might be, or however specific one defines it, sometimes it is helpful to understand what it is not. Imagine for a moment if you could describe any tangible thing that does not have a structure. It is reasonably apparent that if it exists, it has a structure.

The Torah is a written, tangible document that has a structural framework that can be observed by anyone who has a trained eye and the means to examine it.

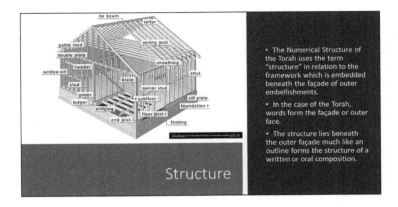

- The Numerical Structure of the Torah uses the term "structure" in relation to the framework which is embedded beneath the façade of outer embellishments.

- In the case of the Torah, words form the façade or outer face.

- The structure lies beneath the outer façade much like an outline forms the structure of a written or oral composition.

Structure

It is often assumed that the Torah is a product of the evolutionary, spiritual insights of the ancient Hebrews. That assumption is not vocalized anywhere in the Torah. Those are the assumptions of men. The doctrine of scriptural *inspiration* is an intellectually shrouded assault upon the author of the Torah, the Creator. Perhaps, the significance of the embedded numerical structure of the Torah may place a formidable impediment in their path. They will never be silenced. Like the pharaoh of the exodus event, they shall continue to rebel against the Creator and reject His instructions, amid whatever astonishing reality may come to pass, to their demise.

For the one who seeks the Creator, the intricacies of the numerical structure of the Torah shall be a formidable defense. If the structure of the Torah is a different aspect of the Torah from the embellishments, then to only investigate the adornments of the Torah would be like only seeing, hearing, or observing half of the Torah. In a similar path of thinking, to ignore or reject the structure would be like neglecting or rejecting half of the Torah. Without the roots, trunk, limbs, branches, stems, and blossoms, the fruit of a tree would not exist.

Consonants

The Hebrew alphabet has only consonants, unlike the English alphabet, which includes the vowels a, e, i, o, u as letters. The ancient texts of the Torah are comprised of consonants only.

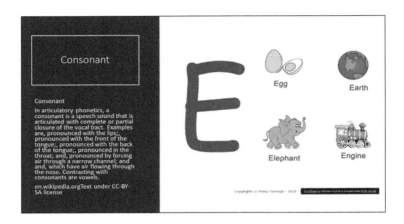

These consonants are initial sound formations, and they require the breath of a vowel to complete their sound. The sounds of the Torah were orally transmitted from the time of Moses until the Masoretic scribes encoded a system around the text, which would not interfere with the integrity of the text. The world owes a great debt to the faithful scribes of Israel, for the preservation of this divine document. Without the conservation of this intricate sound system, it would not be possible to embrace the numerical structure of the Torah.

Ordinal Numbers

The ordinal numbers are related to their position in an array of numbers, such as first (1st), second (2nd), third (3rd), and so forth. The Hebrew alphabet has twenty-two ordinals/consonants in a set specific order; each one of those consonants has a fixed ordinal position. *Aleph* (א) is first, and *tav* (ת) twenty-second is last.

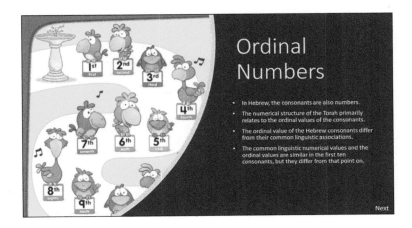

The numerical structure of the Torah is reliant upon the ordinal values of the consonant letters. On the other hand, the disciplines of gematria and numerology are dependent on their alphabetic or literary values. That being the case, all three disciplines agree on the first ten ordinal/consonant numerical values. The significance of the number ten, in the context of Torah, will be worthy of future observation and contemplation.

A Torah Vessel

This terminology is precisely one of those incidents where the author's use of a word may be perplexing to the uninformed reader. A vessel is a container; however, to this writer, a vessel is both a container and vehicle of knowledge. This writer comes from a maritime background, historically, geographically, and vocationally.

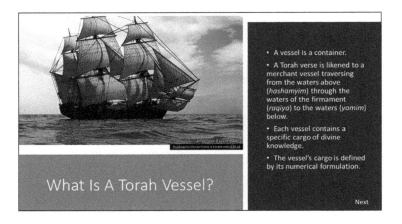

Perhaps, the Creator uses what he has on hand to work with, or maybe it is of divine design. In any case, this has become the model and a good one at that. Herein, a Torah verse shall be referred to as a sailing vessel commissioned in the waters above (the heavens) and navigating the firmament (the mid-waters) to the seas of the earth (the waters below). Each vessel has a specific numerical cargo, and the formulation of that cargo expresses a numerical structure that relays the divine instructions from above to the reader. By this writer's reckoning, there are 5,846 vessels of knowledge in the Torah, and each one of those vessels has been counted three times, cataloged, categorized, and entered into a database. That was a formidable and rewarding task that unequivocally validated the existence of an embedded numerical structure.

Context

The Hebrew language relies heavily on context, and following the context requires careful listening. It is this writer's opinion that context is best described by the word *surroundings*. When something is removed from its surroundings, it becomes isolated, and it stands alone and void of its habitat.

One of the first tools of abuse that is used to marginalize the words of another is to take them out of their context. Politicians are masters of this craft. Sadly, theologians and preachers often place doctrinal precepts before textual surroundings, and thereby either willingly or not, abandon the textual truths.

Context is the heart and soul of truth; however, every reader, translator, and interpreter of scripture is distracted by their collective foreknowledge. The immediate context of a matter is situational, and while situations can be similar, they are not always identical.

The numerical structure of the Torah is a parallel tool which the Creator has provided for the reader to follow his path of thought throughout the matter, without abandoning the context.

Maqaph

When thinking of the relationship between the Torah and the *maqaph*, a Hebrew hyphen, one can only imagine submitting a writing composition to an editor with over fourteen percent of the words being hyphenated. One can only assume that the editor would question the need for all those hyphens, especially when the rules of grammar might only justify a minimal amount of them. There are well over 11,000 *maqaphim* (hyphens) in the Torah text, and few grammarians question why. It is this writer's opinion that there are no insignificant items in the Torah, and that the humble *maqaph* is undoubtedly a welcome guest therein.

The Hebrew *maqaph* joins two or more words together as one word. When the multiple words are linked together, sometimes the vowels may change, and apparently, all the linked words were meant to sound like one word, in one breath. Here is an example of four Hebrew words being joined into one word and spoken in one breath:

עַל־כָּל־דְּבַר־פֶּשַׁע. *Ahl-kahl-devar-pehshahng* (in one breath, please.)

What is interesting is that while the rules concerning the Hebrew vowels are maintained in these compound words; also, the individual integrity of each word is maintained. The above can be proven by the fact that words having the final form of a consonant keep that final form even though they are no longer the final consonant of the newly compounded word.

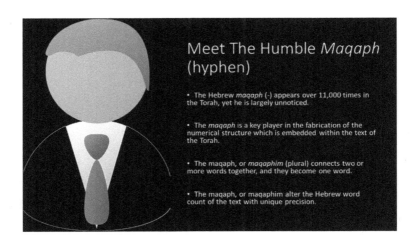

Meet The Humble *Maqaph* (hyphen)

- The Hebrew *maqaph* (-) appears over 11,000 times in the Torah, yet he is largely unnoticed.

- The *maqaph* is a key player in the fabrication of the numerical structure which is embedded within the text of the Torah.

- The maqaph, or *maqaphim* (plural) connects two or more words together, and they become one word.

- The maqaph, or *maqaphim* alter the Hebrew word count of the text with unique precision.

The *maqaphim* presents a unique dilemma when it comes to counting the words of the Hebrew text. According to this researcher's reckoning, there are 79,964 original Hebrew words in the Torah text. The introduction of 11,476 *maqaphim* reduces that word count to a final Hebrew word count of 68,505 words. The question that comes to mind is, what is the real word count? Perhaps, the Creator purposely desired that there should be two separate word counts. Please, realize that the counting of these words was done manually, and there might be some slight human errors, but the overall findings are overwhelming.

The presence of over 11,000 *maqaphim* coupled with the two separate word counts provides a numerical scenario of enormous opportunities that can expand one's understanding of the Torah solely from the Creator's perspective.

Original Text

Concerning the next three terms, the second vessel of the testimony, also known as the Ten Words or Ten Commandments, shall be used for illustration. As previously discussed, there can be two separate word counts of Hebrew words within the vessel's text.

Not all vessels or verses have two different word counts, and these vessels are reckoned to be absolute, having one specific meaning which requires no further guidance by the Creator. There are about 1,000 plus such containers of knowledge. However, the majority, or over 4,800 vessels, have two distinct word counts. Each of these vessels began with a specific word count, which is herein referred to as the original text.

In the text model on the right, the original text has seven Hebrew words. However, the Creator chose to modify this text by inserting two *maqaphim*, thereby altering the Hebrew word count.

The original word count of seven Hebrew words can be linked with the seventh numerical principle to form the foundational meaning of this text.

Modifications

Again, as stated above, changes were made to most of the Torah vessels when the Creator inserted a *maqaph*, thereby altering the Hebrew word count. The first question that came to the researcher's mind was, what is the purpose of the multitude of modifications? Are they grammatically necessary?

Research, through observation, seems to indicate that these modifications were strategically placed as a matter of emphasis, to direct the reader's attention to what is critical to the reader's understanding of the Creator's perspective.

The two modifications can also be linked with the second numerical principle to form the core meaning of this text.

Final Text

The original text of seven Hebrew words has been altered utilizing two modifications. The final Hebrew word count is now five. This can also be linked with the fifth numerical principle to form the closing meaning of this text.

Notice that this vessel has a numerical formulation (7-2-5). This formulation is not a formula for calculation; it is an array of numbers that can be used to classify this vessel. There are forty-six vessels in the Torah which have this same numerical formulation.

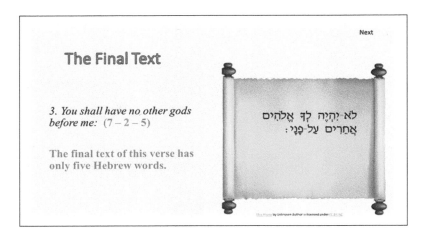

The third numerical principle is related to an encounter with the Creator. Take note that every vessel that the Creator modifies has the formulation of *three* numerical values. The Creator's perspective in this vessel is founded on three principles. Therefore, proper understanding and interpretation should be based upon and congruent with those three principles.

Connections

Making connections add meaning and purpose to life. The more connected one is with life, the less likely one shall engage in any activity which would diminish life, or more severely take or abandon life.

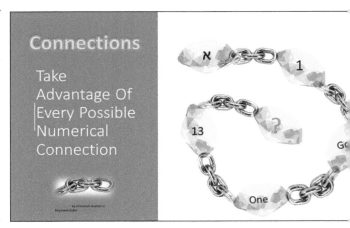

Making positive connections is a healthy endeavor. The Creator spoke concerning the man that He had created, stating it was not good (functional) for him to be alone. There are physical dimensions and spiritual dimensions that man must consider. Adam intimately knew his Father on a spiritual level; however, on the physical level, he had to be led to discover on his own, that no other creature could be related too similarly. After Adam had realized that principle, the Creator formed a suitable mate for him to connect. Adam was so enamored with this new connection that he hearkened to the words of his wife rather than the words of his Father. As a result, his relationship with his Father diminished drastically.

The connections, as discussed herein, are related to enhancing one's relationship with the Father of his soul for the benefit of one's well-being. This book is all about numerical connections which shall strengthen one's understanding of his third parent.

Pattern

A pattern can be associated with a regularity. Patterns are predictable rather than random and unpredictable. Textual critics are generally quick to focus on the randomness of events.

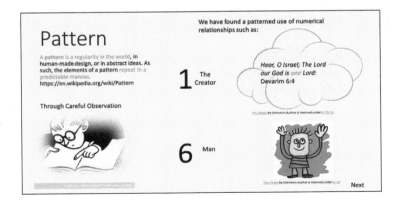

The whole of the Torah text is more likely to be viewed as random events that have naturally occurred in an evolutionary process. Similar to the conventional view of creation, a series of random, unorchestrated events that have produced such spectacular phenomena, which, ironically, can only be analyzed with principled methods.

Patterns are found throughout the whole of creation. They are the reflection of a designer. It is fitting that the Torah should involve patterns as well.

Principle

The word principle is associated with value, and value is associated with worth. Unfortunately, the terms principle, value, and worth are most often related to money. Some of the essential things pertaining to life cannot be purchased with money. Among them are terms such as respect, forgiveness, righteousness, repentance, love, and so on. However, all those terms have principles, value, and worth. It is those types of principles that are the goal of our focus. All these terms have underlying principles that may or may not be explicitly expressed.

Is there a model from which the unwritten principles of these terms may have come about? Perhaps, some principles were in place before creation. It is indeed established, in the writer's opinion, that there were certain principles in place before the communication of the Torah to Moses in the wilderness. The numerical structure of the Torah is all about ten principles.

Please bear in mind that this writer is a pioneer on the path of discovery. Others shall follow who shall see some things more clearly than the trailblazer, and that is good. That being the case, these ten principles are the best that the trailblazer could do considering the confusion of the journey. The trail is blazed, awaiting those to establish the highway.

CHAPTER ONE

What Is the Numerical Structure of The Torah?

It Is a Facet of the Torah Gemstone

While the numerical structure is not the only facet of the Torah, it is perhaps, the most prominent facet, because it was the first to be fashioned by the Creator. It appears to have been the most brilliant part of the stone from which the master began his design.

The numerical structure is only one facet of the Torah gemstone, but perhaps, it is the foremost facet which clearly reflects the beauty of the gemstone.

Come, let's examine the beauty of this multi-faceted gemstone.

Structure Is Found Everywhere.

Where can one look that structure cannot be found? Just think for a moment about atoms, protons, electrons, neutrons, or perhaps, DNA. Structure is an integral part of the totality of our surroundings.

The Torah Is No Different.

If structure is found everywhere, then it should not surprise one that structure also permeates the Torah. The structure of the Torah is nothing new; it has always been there. Much like a literary outline which lies beneath a quality composition, there is a numerical structure embedded within the Torah text.

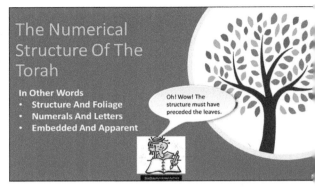

This illustration of a tree's structure, which lies beneath the foliage, can be likened to the Torah's numerical structure. A good question that one might ask is, why has this structure not been discussed by other scholars? Perhaps the adage, "they did not see the forest, because of the trees" applies here.

The Hebrew Ordinals/Consonants Have a Value

Every consonant in the Hebrew alphabet has a numerical value. Then what is the value of an ordinal/consonant? Well, the first ten ordinals/consonants have three valuations. The three assessments might be likened to categories of apples, pears, and bananas. First, their ordinal value (apples), second, their principle value (pears), and third, their literary or gematria value (bananas). The second set of twelve ordinals/consonants has only two valuations: (1) ordinal value (apples) and (2) literary or gematria value (bananas). Therefore, the numerical worth or value of each consonant depends upon which list is being addressed.

The numerical structure of the Torah is primarily concerned with the first two of the three lists: (1) their ordinal value [apples] and (2) their principle value [pears].

THE THREE NUMERICAL VALUATIONS

Ordinal Consonants (Apples)	Ten Principle Consonants (Pears)	Literary/Gematria Consonants (Bananas)
Aleph (א) = 1 or 1st	Aleph (א) = 1st Principle	Aleph (א) = 1 or one
Beit (ב) = 2 or 2nd	Beit (ב) = 2nd Principle	Beit (ב) = 2 or two
Gimmel (ג) = 3 or 3rd	Gimmel (ג) = 3rd Principle	Gimmel (ג) = 3 or three
Dahlet (ד) = 4 or 4th	Dahlet (ד) = 4th Principle	Dahlet (ד) = 4 or four
Heh (ה) = 5 or 5th	Heh (ה) = 5th Principle	Heh (ה) = 5 or five
Vav (ו) = 6 or 6th	Vav (ו) = 6th Principle	Vav (ו) = 6 or six
Zayin (ז) = 7 or 7th	Zayin (ז) = 7th Principle	Zayin (ז) = 7 or seven
Chet (ח) = 8 or 8th	Chet (ח) = 8th Principle	Chet (ח) = 8 or eight
Tet (ט) = 9 or 9th	Tet (ט) = 9th Principle	Tet (ט) = 9 or nine
Yud (י) = 10 or 10th	Yud (י) = 10th Principle	Yud (י) = 10 or ten
Caph (כ) = 11 or 11th		Caph (כ) = 20 or twenty
Lamed (ל) = 12 or 12th		Lamed (ל) = 30 or thirty
Mem (מ) = 13 or 13th		Mem (מ) = 40 or forty
Nun (נ) = 14 or 14th		Nun (נ) = 50 or fifty
Samech (ס) = 15 or 15th		Samech (ס) = 60 or sixty
Gnayin (ע) = 16 or 16th		Gnayin (ע) = 70 or seventy
Peh (פ) = 17 or 17th		Peh (פ) = 80 or eighty
Tzadic (צ) = 18 or 18th		Tzadic (צ) = 90 or ninety
Kuph (ק) = 19 or 19th		Kuph (ק) = 100 or one hundred
Resh (ר) = 20 or 20th		Resh (ר) = 200 or two hundred
Sheen (ש) = 21 or 21st		Sheen (ש) = 300 or three hundred
tav (ת) = 22 or 22nd		tav (ת) = 400 or four hundred

The Ten Numerical Principles in One Word

The purpose of reducing the ten numerical principles to one word for each law is primarily to provide the reader with something easy and tangible to attach to his memory. These single word definitions can readily aid the reader as he casually or intensely reads the Torah text. While one word is efficient, that certainly does not imply that one word is adequate.

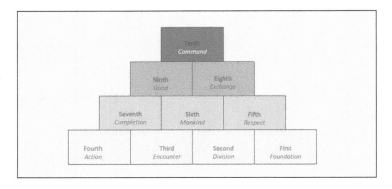

The Ten Numerical Principles in One Statement

The ten principles reflect my judgment over several years of studying the numerical structure of the Torah, they are not, however, set in stone. One must remember that this writer is only a trailblazer in this field of study, and the addition of more exceptional minds, like perhaps yours, shall refine them to a higher degree of accuracy.

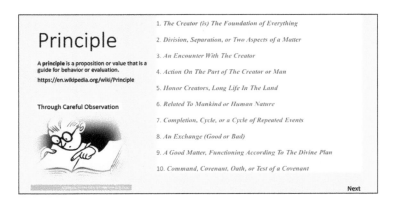

The Numerical Structure Is Relevant to Each Hebrew Consonant.

About four years ago, glimpses of the numerical structure became increasingly apparent, and this writer began to write a commentary on the Hebrew alphabet. After having written numerous pages concerning the first letter, aleph (א), an inner voice informed him that he had begun his study of the alphabet with the wrong consonant. The Torah begins with the ordinal/consonant two (2) or *beit* (ב). As a writer, it is easy to understand the concentrated effort involved in the selection of the first word of a composition. When he investigated the ordinal/consonant *beit* (ב), he realized how significant that inner conversation was. That commentary endeavor has been modified and put on hold in lieu of the urgent nature of the newly found information concerning the embedded numerical structure of the Torah.

Generally, the Hebrew consonants are known by their dictionary definitions, and some also expand the quest by investigating their ancient script characters. Both methods, in this writer's opinion, fall short of the optimal revelation in that they both reflect primarily on the thoughts and actions of man and thereby inadvertently exclude the author's perspective, which is revealed by his patterned usage.

The numerical structure can consistently provide the author's perspective about each consonant if the researcher understands how to find the pattern. In the case of the first ordinal/consonant of the Torah *beit* (ב), the consonant is generally related to the Hebrew word "*bayit*" house. However, the numerical structure implies that the ordinal/consonant should be more precisely related to the concept of "inside."

YouTube channel, "Torah123," has a humorous video presentation specifically addressing the first word and first ordinal/consonant of the Torah.

"Torah123, An Investigation into the Foundation of the Torah"

With the aid of a computer program, one can find the first occurrence of the consonant in the Torah, the first word to begin with the consonant, and the first word to contain the consonant name. One can also find every occurrence of the selected ordinal/consonant as chronologically found in the Torah. After examining the first eighteen occurrences, and extracting the divine pattern of seven selected occurrences, one can relatively understand the divine perspective on the meaning of the consonant.

These two powerful means of understanding the context of a Hebrew consonant, in this writer's opinion, far supersede the scope of the previously mentioned methods.

The Numerical Structure Is Relevant to Clusters of Hebrew Consonants.

A consonant cluster is a sequential array of two or more ordinals/consonants that may or may not constitute an established word. With the aid of a computer program, one can find every occurrence of the selected array of consecutive ordinals/consonants as chronologically found in the Torah. After examining the first eighteen occurrences, and extracting the divine pattern of seven selected occurrences, one can relatively understand the divine perspective on the meaning of the consonant cluster.

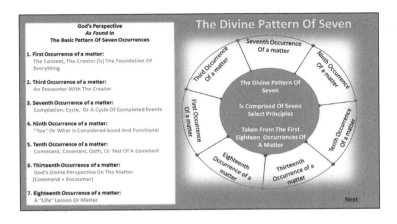

Searching the text utilizing consonant clusters will reveal a multitude of related connections that cannot be achieved through a simple word study or even a word root study.

The Numerical Structure Is Relevant to Each Hebrew Word.

Hebrew words can be searched in the same manner as consonant clusters. Let's look at the Hebrew word *tov* (טוב), which is translated into English as good, according to the ten numerical principles.

THE HEBREW WORD *Tov* (טוב) "GOOD"
ACCORDING TO THE TEN PRINCIPLES

As readers, specifically English readers, it is often assumed an English word corresponds with a Hebrew concept. Unfortunately, Hebrew thought patterns are not always congruent with English thought patterns. The only defense mechanism against erroneous misconceptions, readily available to the reader, is that of context. When one progresses from reading to an investigation, the setting plays an even more significant role. The numerical structure of the Torah is devoted entirely to context. The structure forms the foundation of the context. The ten principles of the numerical structure are the highlighted purple scripts.

First Occurrence: *The Creator (Is) The Foundation of Everything*

Testimony #1:

Ber. 1: 4. *And God saw the light, that it was good; and God divided the light from the darkness:*

> This vessel forms the foundational meaning of *tov* (טוב), but what does the English word *good* mean? Here are some commonly used English synonyms: decent, respectable, moral, upright, virtuous, noble, worthy, blameless, and wholesome. None of the above synonyms seem to fit the context of this vessel of knowledge.
>
> The context appears to be describing something that is functioning as planned. Imagine if this vessel were translated:
>
> *And God saw the light, that it was <u>functional</u>; and God divided the light from the darkness:*
>
> Perhaps, most of our English translations have gotten off to less than a practical understanding of this foundational word. The first ordinal/consonant to begin the Torah is *"beit"* or *"2,"* which relates to division. Dividing the light from the darkness is the first creative action to take place on planet earth.

Second Occurrence: Division, Separation, or Two Aspects of a Matter

Testimony #2:

Ber. 1: 10. *And God called the dry land Earth; and the gathering together of the waters He called Seas; and God saw that it was* good:

> This second occurrence of good certainly relates to the second principle of division or separation or two aspects of a matter. The matter is planet earth, the division or separation has to do with the dry land and the seas.

> Again, the concept of being functional fits well. Perhaps, an even better fit might be *functioning according to the divine plan.*

Third Occurrence: An Encounter with The Creator

Testimony #3:

Ber. 1: 12. *And the earth brought forth grass, and herb yielding seed after its kind, and tree yielding fruit, whose seed was in itself, after its kind; and God saw that it was* good:

> At first glance, one might say, "Where is the encounter?" Grass, herbs, and trees are the early signs of life mentioned concerning the planet. While there may appear to be a scientific clash at this point, one should consider that neither the theologian nor the scientist has all the facts at present. What one can determine from this vessel is that life encountered the planet in the form of plant life, which comes from the Creator.

Fourth Occurrence: Action on The Part of The Creator or Man
Testimony #4:

Ber. 1: 18. *And to rule over the day and over the night, and to divide the light from the darkness; and God saw that it was* good:

> The word rule is an action word, and this action was initiated and maintained by the Creator, which is fitting according to the fourth principle: action on the part of the Creator or man.

Fifth Occurrence: Honor Creators, Long Life in The Land
Testimony #5:

Ber. 1: 21. *And God created the great crocodiles, and every kind of creature that live in the waters, and every kind of winged birds, and God saw that it was* good: (23-4-19)

> There are times when one cannot be certain as to how to apply an ordinal principle to the vessel; however, this is where the structure of the vessel comes into play. This vessel's numerical formulation is (23-4-19), meaning this vessel began with twenty-three words; it was modified four times, and it now has a final word count of nine-teen words.
>
> (23-4-19)

23   *Command;* combined with *Covenant, Oath, or Test of a Covenant;* combined with *An Encounter with The Creator*

4   *Action on The Part of The Creator or Man*

19   *Command, Covenant, Oath, or Test of a Covenant;* combined with *A Good Matter, Functioning According to The Divine Plan*

This vessel's overall theme is about respect for the Creator. The foundation of this vessel is three-fold: (1) the Creator created these creatures by means of a command [He commanded the waters]; (2) their creation involved either a covenant, a test of the covenant, or command; (3) this act of creation was an encounter with the Creator.

The core meaning of this vessel is related to action on the part of the Creator.

The ultimate meaning is related to the command becoming a functional matter. Note that these creatures span from the depths to the heights of the earth. Therefore, the Creator is honored throughout the earth's environs.

Sixth Occurrence: *Related to Mankind or Human Nature*

Testimony #6:

Ber. 1: 25. *And God made the beasts of the earth after their kind, and cattle after their kind, and everything that creeps upon the earth after its kind; and God saw that it was good:*

All these creatures share the dry land with humanity.

Seventh Occurrence: *Completion, Cycle, or A Cycle of Repeated Events*

Testimony #7:

Ber. 1: 31. *And God saw everything that he had made,*

The words "everything that he had made" imply that the creative acts were completed, and these creations keep cycling repeatedly.

Eighth Occurrence: An Exchange (Good or Bad)
Testimony #8:

Ber. 2:9. *And out of the ground made the Lord God every tree to grow that is pleasant to the sight, and good for food; the tree of life also in the midst of the garden, and the tree of knowledge of good and evil:*

> The exchange here involves the fruit which functionally sustains life, however, there was one tree that had a mixed nature of fruit that was both good and evil. Therefore, the exchange could be good (functional) or evil (dysfunctional).

Ninth Occurrence: A Good Matter, Functioning According to The Divine Plan
Testimony #9:

Ber. 2: 9. *And out of the ground made the Lord God every tree to grow that is pleasant to the sight, and **good** for food; the tree of life also in the midst of the garden, and the tree of knowledge of good and evil:*

> The possibility of man's failure was part of the plan for man. There is an easy way and a hard way, but the choice was man's choice. Disobedience and evil walk hand in hand, and their outcomes are dysfunctional.

Tenth Occurrence: Command, Covenant, Oath, Test of a Covenant
Testimony #10:

Ber. 2: 12. *And the gold of that land is* good*; there is bdellium and the onyx stone:*

This vessel has eight Hebrew words, and eight relates to an exchange (good or bad). In this case, the exchange would have been good, consisting of gold, bdellium, and onyx stone. However, the reward for disobedience was death, pain, thorns, and thistles, and the first couple's disobedience brought them a dysfunctional outcome.

THE HEBREW WORD *Tov* (טוֹב) "GOOD" ACCORDING TO ITS ORDINALS/CONSONANTS

As an English researcher with limited Hebrew linguistic skills, one can investigate the author's perspective on any given Hebrew word found in the Torah. The following is an example of a simple numerical investigation into the Hebrew word tov.

- The Hebrew word tov (טוֹב) can also be examined consonant by consonant.

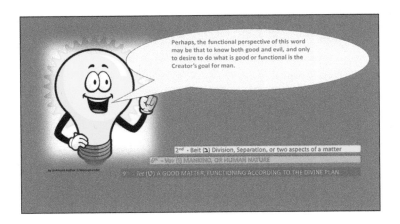

- Tov (טוב) can also be viewed as 9th ordinal + 6th ordinal + 2nd ordinal = 17. *Tov* begins with the ninth ordinal (*tet*, ט) followed by the sixth ordinal (*vav*, ו) and closes with the second ordinal (*beit*, ב). These ordinals demonstrate the natural progression of thought in the fabrication of this Hebrew word.

9th - 6th - 2nd Ordinal Principles

9   *A Good Matter, Functioning According To The Divine Plan*

6   *Related To Mankind or Human Nature*

2   *Division, Separation, or Two Aspects of a Matter*

The Numerical Structure Is Relevant to Each Hebrew Vessel.

One can study any matter that is discussed in multiple vessels in the same passage since, generally, the divine matter will follow the ten numerical principles concerning a matter.

The Numerical Structure Is Relevant to Each Hebrew Book and Chapter of the Torah

The five books of the Torah follow the divine numerical pattern; up to five, of course.

The Five Books According to The Numerical Principles
First Book: *Bereshiyt* (Genesis)
First Principle: The Creator is the foundation of every created thing.
Second Book: *Shemot* (Exodus)
Second Principle: Division, separation, or two aspects of a matter
Third Book: *VaYikra* (Leviticus)
Third Principle: An encounter with the Creator
Fourth Book: *BeMidbar* (Numbers)
Fourth Principle: Action on the part of the Creator, man, or both
Fifth Book: *Devarim* (Deuteronomy)
Fifth Principle: Honor and respect for one's creators

What Then, Is the Numerical Structure?

The numerical structure of the Torah is founded upon ten principles. These ten principles underlie the whole of the Torah structure. Perhaps these ten principles preexist creation.

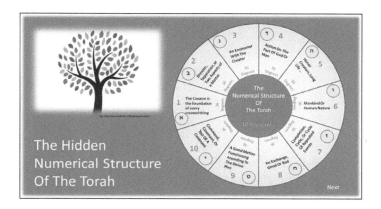

It Is Observable by All Who Are Willing to Look for It.

The numerical structure is not solely the domain of an elite group. It is available to every reader with a minimum of tools, and the mastery of a few necessary skills.)

CHAPTER TWO

What Is the Numerical Structure of a Verse?

An Absolute Vessel.

The first vessel of the Torah is an absolute vessel meaning that the Creator has not modified it utilizing the insertion of a *maqaph*. Since it has not been modified, it is considered as absolutely providing all the information that the Creator deemed necessary. According to this researcher's reckoning, there are one thousand eighteen (1,018) absolute vessels out of five thousand eight-hundred forty-six (5,846) vessels in the Torah. That translates to only about seventeen percent of the Torah vessels are absolute or unmodified by the Creator. The flip side of the coin is that eighty-three percent of the Torah vessels have been modified by the Creator to accentuate their meaning according to the Creator's perspective.

A Modified Vessel.

Torah vessels are modified using a Hebrew *maqaph*, which is like an English hyphen. According to this researcher's reckoning, there are over 11,400 *maqaphim* found in the Torah text. Grammatically speaking, there is certainly no rule related requirement, which could justify over 11,400 *maqaphim*. Perhaps one should ask why so many *maqaphim* are present in the Torah text. One vessel of the Torah, *Shemot* (Exod. 22:8), has thirty-one Hebrew words with eleven *maqaphim*; the *maqaphim* comprise thirty-five percent of this vessel. One must ask, what is going on here?

The first vessel of the Torah (Ber. 1:1) is absolute, having seven unmodified Hebrew words. However, the second vessel of the Torah (Ber. 1:2) has undergone modification. Originally, the second vessel of the Torah consisted of fourteen Hebrew words, and it was modified twice utilizing two *maqaphim*; therefore, this second vessel now has a new word count of twelve Hebrew words.

Visually Comparing the Two Types of Vessels.

One of the critical skills of mastering numerical research is being able to recognize if a vessel has been modified. While the skill is simple enough, it does require visual concentration and mental discipline to verify each *maqaph*, which may often be camouflaged within the text. The graphic illustration below is a comparison of the first two vessels of the Torah.

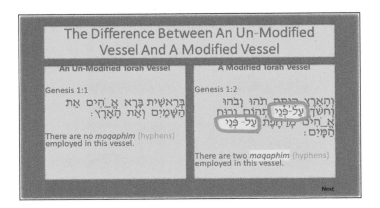

A Vessel's Formulation.

Every Torah vessel has a numerical formulation of three numerical facts. The first fact is derived by the amount of the original Hebrew words which are contained within the vessel $(14 - x - x)$. The second fact is derived from the amount of *maqaphim* found in the vessel (x – 2 – x). The third fact is derived from the final Hebrew word count contained within the vessel (x – x – 12). Therefore, the vessel's formulation is (14 – 2 – 12).

In the case of an absolute vessel containing fourteen Hebrew words, the formulation would be (14 – 0 – 14).

A Vessel's Path of Understanding.

There is a repetitive path of understanding which can be followed to gain insight into the Creator's perspective. You don't have to be a documented biblical scholar, rabbi, or theologian to stop and smell the roses along the path. While all three of them can provide valuable insights and should by no means be ignored, the exceptional value of the numerical structure is that it allows for contextual guidance. The numerical structure is the foundational element of the context, and context is related to reading comprehension. While this skill can lead to better interpretations, it is primarily a reading comprehension tool, which was purposefully placed within the text so that the Creator's message would be less likely to be taken out of context. Follow the signposts on the path of understanding and experience the Creator's hand guiding you along the way.

The Path of Understanding

"Thus says the Lord, Stand on the roads, and see, and ask for the old paths, where the good way is, and walk there, and you shall find rest for your souls..." (Jer. 6:16).

CHAPTER THREE

What Is the Significance of These Verse Formulations?

The Proof Is in the Pudding.

For many years I have heard and used this adage, and like most things, the original meaning is lost to our time. Thanks to the word detective at word-detective.com, perhaps the true meaning has been resurrected. Please visit the website for the rest of the story. In any event, the pudding analogy here is intended to bring to the reader's awareness of how prolifically the numerical structure is embedded within the Torah text. Many more versions of the pudding wait to be discovered and savored. Here are six of the versions that have been brought to the table. The chef says, "Try it; you'll like it! It is good, and it is healthy! Don't be shy; give it a try!"

The proof is in the pudding.

At first glance, "the proof is in the pudding" seems thoroughly mysterious. What proof, in what pudding? Does this have anything to do with Colonel Mustard in the study with a candlestick? But the key to the mystery lies in the fact that "the proof is in the pudding" is actually a mangled form of the original phrase, which was "the proof of the pudding is in the eating." A dish may have been made from a good recipe with fresh ingredients and look delicious, but you can really only judge it by putting it in your mouth. The actual taste is the only true criterion of success.

www.word-detective.com/2008/12/the-proof-is-in-the-pudding/

Alphabet Pudding

The Hebrew alphabet can be investigated with fantastic results, utilizing the numerical structure.

Consonant Cluster Pudding

Consonant clusters are only partial representations of words. When consonant clusters are investigated according to the numerical structure, the same amazing results shall be manifested. Surprising word connections will be revealed.

Word Pudding

When the numerical structure is employed in conjunction with traditional word study methods, the depths of word knowledge and textual relationships shall be astonishing.

Sentence and Vessel Pudding

A simple, brief exercise that can immediately display the significance of the numerical structure of the Torah concerning the order of vessels in a Torah matter is to apply the ten principles to the first ten vessels of the Torah. They will clearly follow the numerical pattern.

Chapter Pudding

Another exciting application of the numerical structure is to apply the ten principles to the first ten chapters of the Torah. Again, they will clearly follow the numerical pattern.

Book Pudding

The book of *Bereshiyt* (Gn.) is the foundation.

The book of *Shemot* (Ex.) is about the division of the nation of Israel from the other nations.

The book of *VaYikra* (Lev.) is about how to encounter the Creator in holiness.

The book of *BeMidbar* (Nu.) is about the actions of the people of Israel and the Creator.

The book of *Devarim* (Dt.) is about respect for the commands of the Creator.

The Mindful (Remember) Pudding

Several years before the numerical structure of the Torah came to light, I cataloged and categorized all the passages in the Torah, where the Torah instructed the general population of the people of Israel to *remember*. It was an enlightening study which formed a "Cliff Note" type of a synopsis of what the Creator considered to be essential points to remember. I concluded that there were thirteen categories of things to remember.

A few years later, as the numerical structure became the focus of my studies, I was astonished to see how these thirteen categories followed the numerical structure of the Torah.

Two Dishes of Commandment (Testimony) Pudding

The ten commandments, or more precisely "ten words" are presented twice in the Torah, each being similar, yet the latter contains a bit more details, or colloquially speaking, more fine print. However, each of these presentations is comprised of thirteen vessels. Likewise, each of these presentations follows the numerical structure of the Torah.

The Shema (Listen) Pudding

The "Shema" (Dev. 6:4-9) passage is one of the most sacred passages of the Torah in the Jewish religion, and this holy passage follows the numerical structure as well.

Validation

The twenty-two consonants validate the numerical structure of the Torah. The nearly eighty thousand Hebrew words testify of the numerical structure, along with the eleven thousand plus *maqaphim*. Five thousand four hundred and eighty-six Torah vessels bear witness of the same testimony concerning the numerical structure of the Torah. Is any further validation required to establish a repetitive numerical pattern?

An Introduction to a Divine Conversation

Lexicons, commentaries, traditions, homilies, and other outside sources have their place, and they all have one thing in common, they are the product of man's rational thinking. Only the Torah is the breath of the Creator; to the rejecters of Torah, this is inconceivable, and no amount of truth will shatter their pharaonic hearts. By examining the structure embedded in the Torah, one encounters the thoughts behind the words and experiences an ongoing conversation with the Creator. Imagine following the views of the Creator as he spoke the words of the Torah to Moses, the scribe. The reader should be aware that he is now able to participate in that initial Torah conversation atop Mount Sinai.

What outside source of Torah information can ascend to the actual words of life, much less at the source of their commencement? This facet of the Torah text is my Father's (*Avi*) Hebrew. These thought patterns are my Father's thoughts. If we so desire and seek, we can be privy to this marvelous conversation. Why? Because that is His desire for you and me. Blessed are you, *HaShem*.

Provides a Reading Comprehension Strategy

As a teacher, who taught reading skills for seven years, it was an astonishing discovery to find that there are reading comprehension strategies embedded throughout the Torah text. What text can be compared to the Torah? What other documents have such strategies consistently embedded in every aspect of the texts?

Provides a Contextual Roadmap

From the first ordinal/consonant to the first word, to the first vessel, to the first chapter, to the first book, to the final book, to the last word, and the last ordinal/consonant; there is a numerical roadmap to guide the reader throughout the journey.

Perhaps, this Torah is far more intricate than you ever imagined. Probably, this Torah is more understandable than you ever thought. You don't need to buy this roadmap. The Creator provided it for you, and the faithful scribes of Israel have preserved it for you.

Happy Motoring!

Provides the Ability to Compare and Contrast

The primary significance of these different verse formulations is that they can be compared with similar vessels having a common numerical fact or facts. Each vessel's numerical formulation or array presents a sequence of values.

SOME EXAMPLES OF WHAT ONE CAN COMPARE

All the verses that begin with:
Three Hebrew words - 14 vessels
Seven Hebrew words - 239 vessels
Seventeen Hebrew words - 334 vessels

All the verses that these modifications:
Zero modifications - 1,018 vessels (Absolute Vessels)
One modification - 1,622 vessels
Eleven modifications - 1 vessel

All the verses that end with:
One final word - 0 vessels
Two final words - 2 vessels
Ten final words - 509 vessels

CHAPTER FOUR

Why Are there Ten Foundational Principles of the Numerical Structure?

Why Are There Ten Foundational Principles?

That is a great question that exceeds my limited knowledge, but perhaps the best strategical approach might be that of adding some questions to the question.

WHY ARE THERE TEN FOUNDATIONAL NUMERICAL PRINCIPLES?

1. Why are there ten sayings expressing the six creative days?
2. Why do we have ten toes, five on the right and five on the left?
3. Why do we have ten fingers, five on the right and five on the left?
4. Why are there ten generations from Adam to Noach?
5. Why are there ten generations from Shem to Abram?
6. Why did Sarah offer Hagar to bear Abraham children after ten years in the land of Canaan?
7. Why does the first vessel to have ten absolute words (10-0-10) refer to Abram and Sarah?
8. Why did Abraham plead that possibly there were ten righteous men in Sodom?

9. Why is the word ten mentioned three times in connection with Rebekah's marriage covenant?
10. What is so significant about Jacob's wages being changed ten times?
11. Why did the divine judgment upon Egypt consist of ten plagues?
12. Why are there ten words in the testimony of the covenant?
13. Why are there ten curtains in the Tabernacle?

The Significance of Ten in the Torah

All the above, unanswered questions unquestionably imply that the Creator deems the number ten to be of great significance. What is interesting is that if one combines all the questions above, they total fourteen questions. Fourteen is related to (10) a command, or a test of a command, combined with (4) action on the part of the Creator or man.

Ten being the foundation of this matter is related to a command; a command implies the speech of a commander, and the declaration of a commander suggests a continuation of the commander's thoughts.

Now concerning the four, it is related to action on the part of the Creator. Perhaps, there are four specific actions to be associated with this matter. The first being the ten principles, the second being the ten sayings of creation, the third being the ten terms (words) of the testimony of the covenant, and the fourth being the test.

The Ten Principles – Action #1

Based on years of research concerning the numerical structure of the Torah, it is this researcher's opinion that the ten numerical principles precede the creative actions of the first six days. Creation had to begin with a plan; a plan requires disciplined thought, and disciplined thinking requires prerequisite principles. We afford respect to a person when we refer to them as a *person of principles*. How much more should we consider the Creator as a *being of principles?*

Undoubtedly, these fundamental principles that have been put forth herein shall undergo a refinement process, in my thinking, as well as in the thoughts of other capable persons. At present, however, they do provide a platform from which to labor.

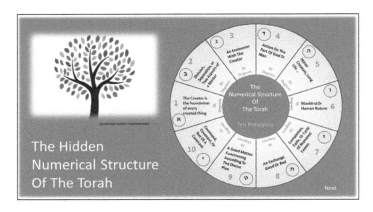

The Ten Sayings of Creation – Action #2

One might say that it is merely a coincidence that the first chapter of the Torah, which describes the six days of creation, repetitively states, "And God said," ten times. Again, it is this writer's opinion that these ten sayings stem from the preceding ten numerical principles, which motivate the Creator.

Modern-day science suggests that from a random explosive act, the whole of this intricately designed universe developed from perpetually positive accidental actions. Wow! In which laboratory have they been able to reproduce such random behavior even on a minuscule scale? The rationality of such behavior pales in the light of the numerical structure of the Torah, as presented herein.

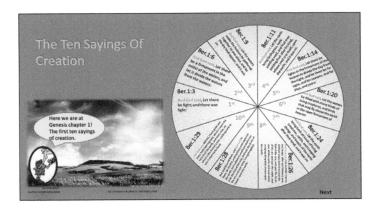

The Ten Words of the Testimony – Action #3

Perhaps some shall be "offended" by this next set of assertions, that is not to say that anything herein is designed to be offensive. But literally, some readers may be *off*, *ended*, or caught startlingly off-balance.

The Torah is eternal; however, it should be acknowledged that some hold unrealistic beliefs concerning the concept of a new Torah. The Torah itself does not appear to ever hint at its demise.

The prophet says that the Creator shall put his Torah in their inward parts; he will write his Torah in their hearts. Where in the Torah or the prophets is one told about two Torahs? Perhaps, if one believed in two gods, then the concept of two Torahs would follow suit. One needs other sources outside of the Torah and the prophets to propagate such propositions.

Anyone who teaches a doctrine that is contrary to the Torah should be labeled a false teacher, according to the Torah. However, the Creator permitted the false teacher to exist; because the false teacher is designed to test the obedience of the Creator's servants.

The Ten Words are the testimony concerning the covenant between the Creator and Israel, the firstborn of the nations. Israel, as the firstborn, has a responsibility to teach the Torah to the other sons, or nations of the world. That Torah contains the ten words of the testimony.

The interesting fact about the ten words is that they were given to a mixed multitude of people outside the land of promise. One can keep those commands outside of the land of promise. They are and shall be *universal.*

There are not any one of these commands that cannot be observed by a non-Israelite. Non-Israelites followed them in the wilderness for forty years. These ten words are a testimony of the condition of one's relationship with the Creator. If one rejects any of these commands, he is giving proof that he rejects the covenant.

The whole world shall be filled with His glory, despite Israel's short-comings and mankind's rejection of Torah. In some future time, what the prophet Jeremiah spoke shall come to pass, and the world shall begin to learn Torah and keep the Sabbath of the Creator. Then, humanity shall once again obediently commence fulfilling the *great commission* of Ber. 1:28.

The Prophet Jeremiah Speaks About The "New Covenant" (31:30-34)

Foundation

30. *Behold, the days come, says the Lord, that I will make a new covenant with the house of Israel, and with the house of Judah:*

Division, Separation

31. *Not according to the covenant that I made with their fathers in the day that I took them by the hand to bring them out of the land of Egypt; my covenant which they broke, although I was their master, says the Lord:*

An Encounter

32. *But this shall be the covenant that I will make with the house of Israel; After those days, says the Lord, I will put my Torah in their inward parts, and write it in their hearts; and will be their God, and they shall be my people:*

Action

33. *And they shall teach no more every man his neighbor, and every man his brother, saying, Know the Lord; for they shall all know me, from the least of them to the greatest of them, says the Lord; for I will forgive their iniquity, and I will no longer remember their sin:*

And God blessed them, and God said to them, Be fruitful, and multiply, and replenish the earth, and subdue it; and have dominion over the fish of the sea, and over the birds of the air, and over every living thing that moves upon the earth:

These Ten Words are a daily encounter with the Creator. They are a testimony of acceptance or rejection on the part of man. Only the Creator can distinguish between ignorance and rebellion, and apparently, He has a point from which He draws the line of separation. These Ten Words and the Torah have been schlepped the world over by Jews and Christians. While one's claim of ignorance may seem plausible, perhaps it may not be sustainable before the judge of the world.

Religions possess the same dynamics as individuals; they can be prone to lean toward their self-interest, rather than that of their Creator's. In defense of the nation of Israel, they were called to a level of holiness for which there is no match, and more precisely, this level of holiness, even though it is national, hung on the balance of individual behavior. When one Israelite, such as Achan, transgresses the commands, the whole nation suffers (Josh. 7:1).

> But the people of Israel committed a trespass in regard to the devoted property, for Achan, the son of Carmi, the son of Zabdi, the son of Zerah, of the tribe of Judah, took of the devoted things; and the anger of the Lord was kindled against the people of Israel:

How, one might ask, shall the nation of Israel be able to live according to this standard of holiness? Well, that is what the prophet Jeremiah was communicating. The Creator would perform an inside operation in the hearts (the seat of intellect, not the place of emotion) of all Israel. Is this rational in terms of the Torah? Yes, because long ago, the Creator performed a similar internal operation and changed every man's speech during the construction of the tower of Babel.

These ten words should not be taken lightly.

Ten Represents the Test or Testing — Action #4

Remember those previously mentioned questions:

Why did Abram plead that possibly there were ten righteous men in Sodom?

> Perhaps, he intuitively knew that there was a bottom line, and he assumed that line to be ten. Maybe, he thought that there were ten members in Lot's family and believed them to be righteous. Whatever the case may be, ten in this passage is related to divine judgment.

Why is the word ten mentioned three times in connection with Rebekah's marriage covenant?

> Perhaps, the ten laden camels, and ten-shekel bracelets, and the ten days to consider the matter of the marriage were what it would take to judge the covenant as a genuine proposition.

What is so significant about Jacob's wages being changed ten times?

Did Jacob consider the ten times to be enough to determine the intent of Laban? Jacob certainly seemed to act upon the tenth occurrence of this transgression.

Why did the divine judgment upon Egypt consist of ten plagues?

The whole of Egypt did not react to the tenth plague in a unified manner. Pharaoh rejected each of the plagues to his demise. Many of the Egyptians bestowed their wealth upon the Israelites to be done with the plagues. But what is surprising is that a significant number of them followed Israel and the Creator out of Egypt, and very few hold the opinion that the whole of Israel exited Egypt.

The point to be pondered here is that the *ten* is associated with the final determination resting on the individual level. Every acceptor and rejecter made their own choice.

Review

There are ten principles because the Creator chooses to format his actions around the numeral ten. There are too many significant Torah matters that are related to ten to be dismissed. One of the multiple benefits of the numerical structure of the Torah is its ability to connect the researcher to the larger picture and buffer the assault of fragmented theology.

CHAPTER FIVE

What Is the Pattern of the Divine Perspective?

What Is the Divine Perspective?

There are always two perspectives in a divine conversation. The whole of the Torah is a divine conversation which was communicated to Moses for our benefit. However, something that is generally common to all discussions is that most often, people only hear what they want to hear and dismiss or ignore the other parts of the conversation. It is commonly referred to as selective listening, which is merely ignoring the speaker's perspective and filtering the dialogue to fit the listener's perspective.

Selective listeners are generally the proponents of partisan theologies. If there is only one God, why are there so many theologies? In a nutshell, there is one divine source, the Torah, and a multitude of other human-made sources. The other man-made sources present a variety of opinions. The thought among many is that the more views which are considered, the more broadminded one becomes, having viewed a matter from many perspectives? It is usually not regarded as intellectual to be sternly opinionated. Agreeably, it would be tragic to be strongly opinionated and incorrect in the eyes of the Creator. The only safe way to navigate the narrow channel between properly opinionated and improperly opinionated is to know the Creator's perspective.

The three main monotheistic religions: Judaism, Christianity, and Islam, all accept the Torah as a unique book, yet they hold varying opinions about the text. The varying opinions have their roots in man-made perspectives. In this present age, it is highly unlikely that all men shall embrace the Creator's perspective; perhaps in a messianic era, this shall commence changing. However, in the present, it is one individual at a time accomplishment. Herein is a method of study which one can use the numerical structure to investigate the divine perspective on any Torah matter. The divine perspective is a set pattern of seven specific occurrences of a thing, which are found in the first eighteen occurrences of that matter.

Why Does the Divine Perspective Involve Eighteen Occurrences of a Matter?

That is a great question. In the early years of this numerical adventure, certain numbers were assumed to relate to the Creator. Twenty-six at that time was the higher limit and one being the lowest limit, however, a pattern seemed to emerge, and it was concluded that the upper research limit could be reduced to eighteen. The reduction of the search range reduced the research time and streamlined the investigation with no apparent effect on the results. Twenty-six is the ordinal numerical value of the sacred name of the Creator (י_וה), while eighteen is the ordinal numerical value associated with life (חי). In my mind, the divine perspective was a "life" matter.

Why Does the Divine Perspective Have Seven Elements?

During the early years of research concerning the numerical structure, a pattern began to develop around the ordinal seven which seemed to establish a definitive relationship to the concepts of completion and cycle. Seven, according to the numerical structure of the Torah, relates to completion, cycle, or a cycle of repeated events.

Well, if the desire is to continuously be able to find the divine perspective on a Torah matter the process would have to comprise the elements of *completion* and a *continuous cycle* of repeated events. Therefore, like the summary of the creation of the heavens and the earth is summarized in seven Hebrew words *Bereshiyt* (Gn. 1:1); seven was the perfect fit for the task.

A Unique Comparison Concerning the Divine Perspective

The study of gematria is a Kabbalistic method of investigating the Torah according to the literary numerical values of the Hebrew consonants. Thus the "gematria" value of a word or phrase would be the sum of the literary numerical values contained in the word or phrase. There is, in this writer's opinion, an inherent weakness in this investigative method, and that is that two diametrically opposed terms can have the same gematria. While this writer is not skilled in this medium of study, there seems to be another disappointing feature.

In some cases, "close may seem to be close enough," and "close" may be fine in the game of pitching horseshoes. However, accuracy should be the goal of Torah research. Regardless of this writer's criticisms, there are many intriguing and unique things to be discovered utilizing gematria.

Gematria

Gematria is an alphanumeric code of assigning a numerical value to a name, word or phrase based on its letters. A single word can yield multiple values depending on the cipher used.

The numerical structure should not be likened to gematria, because it uses the ordinal values of all the ordinals/consonants, and therefore, it is not connected at all with the literary values. In this method of investigation, close doesn't count; if it fits, it belongs, and if it doesn't fit, it doesn't belong.

Several years after having discovered the divine pattern of seven occurrences which signify the divine perspective on a Torah matter; a unique numerical connection was found to exist concerning the divine pattern, judgment, The Creator, and the great flood.

What Does All This Imply?

This pattern, in the writer's opinion, provides consistent and overwhelming evidence of the divine nature of the Torah. For such a model to be consistently evidenced throughout the entire Torah text, in this writer's opinion, it is beyond the capabilities of man's reasoning and engineering skills. *Baruch Atah HaShem!*

God's Perspective as Found in The Basic Pattern of Seven Occurrences

1. First Occurrence: The Context, The Creator (is) The Foundation of Everything

2. Third Occurrence: An Encounter with The Creator:

3. Seventh Occurrence: Completion, Cycle, or A Cycle of Completed Events:

4. Ninth Occurrence: "Tov" Or What Is Considered Good and Functional:

5. Tenth Occurrence: Command, Covenant, Oath, or Test of a Covenant:

6. Thirteenth Occurrence: God's Divine Perspective on the

7. Eighteenth Occurrence: A "Life" Lesson or Matter:

At the right is the basic pattern of the "seven selected" occurrences found in the first eighteen occurrences of any Hebrew textual matter. This set pattern continually yields a consistent pattern of understanding the Torah from The Creator's perspective; whether it is used for single consonant occurrences, consonant clusters, words, specific word occurrences, or vessels of knowledge.

Literally Speaking

The Creator did not begin his text in the Torah with, "I am God," as one might think he would. Instead, He started his writing literally with these words, "Inside first of, created God...," and not with, "I am God, and this is how I did it all." He does not refer to Himself as "I" in the Torah text until He is about to bring judgment upon the world in the time of Noach.

> Ber. 6:17. *And, behold, I* (אֲנִי), *myself, bring a flood of waters upon the earth, to destroy all flesh, where there is the breath of life, from under heaven; and everything that is in the earth shall die:*

The Creator Is Known for What He "Does."

We generally recognize the Creator as the first and foremost "I," a pronoun, which stands in the place of the noun, Creator. However, the Creator has chosen to be known by His "actions" first, and His teachings second. For example, He introduced Himself to every man, woman, and child of the persons of Israel, at Mount Sinai, as their God who brought them, the people of Israel, out of the land of Egypt. Notice, action first, teaching second. The Hebrew language which the Creator first gave to humankind is built upon a verbal root system.

Caution! Man Is Also Known by His "Actions"

The Ignorant, the Thoughtless, the Careless, and the Rebellious Consider the Creator's Repeated Testimonies As Vain

The Creator has made Himself known to every man in every generation, but His words have been mainly taken in vain. How, you might ask, has He made Himself known to all men of all ages? He has done so through His creative actions. Every man throughout all of mankind's generations has been endowed with a mind that can compare the evidence that is openly laid before him. How can such an intricate universe be the result of accidental occurrences? Is there such evidence to compare the perfection of the whole of creation with the random, progressive events of a non-animated means? A fantastic and intricate design without a designer is like a thoughtless person leaving his world of thought, simply because he never thought about it. One cannot compare without thinking, and to not compare is to be absent of thought in the matter. How a man thinks is directly related to his existence, and thoughtfulness, thoughtlessness, and rebelliousness are merely terms that can describe his current state of life.

There is no such human condition as thoughtlessness, every person thinks, the careless person gives little if any thought to his existence, simply because he doesn't care. Sadly, a well-known scientist spoke concerning the Creator, stating he simply didn't care about the Creator's existence. In a case such as this, one should inquire if there is any difference between carelessness and rebelliousness.

The Divine Judgment of The World

Nonetheless, divine judgment has been executed in past times, and the Creator shall again execute judgment in future times, if mankind continues the cycle of refusing to listen and think. This patterned method of numerical research concerning the pattern related to the divine perspective, as demonstrated below, is devoted to understanding the first "I," and His perspective on the language and teachings of His marvelous Torah. The ignorance, thoughtlessness, carelessness, and rebellious actions of men have enormously erupted again in this modern era, like the pre-flood conditions in the time of Noach. Perhaps the day of the Lord is fast approaching.

The Divine Judgment of The World in The Days of Noach

Conversion and confession are two of the major avenues with which man approaches the possibility of a coming divine judgment. Join this group or confess this faith, and the horrors of divine judgment are alleviated. The rising flood waters of Noach's epic event are widely dismissed as a mythical, ethical treatise propagated by the ignorant ancients. However, if this historic event, as described in the Torah, is taken as a divine instruction concerning a real happening, one might project that there was a considerable amount of conversion and confession taking place as the waters critically arose. How well did those conversion and confession strategies work for that generation once the divine judgment was pronounced? Perhaps, a prior change of actions might have been a better strategy. The recording of this epic flood event provides excellent insight on how to enhance the understanding of one's existence and the Creator's perspective on this and future monumental matters.

The Foundation of The Divine Perspective: "And Behold, I (אָנִי), Myself"

Ber. 6:17. *And, behold, I (אָנִי), myself, bring a flood of waters upon the earth, to destroy all flesh, where there is the breath of life, from under heaven; and everything that is in the earth shall die:*

The Hebrew word for "I" in the scripture passage above, is "*ani*," אֲנִי (ahnee). The pronoun "*ani*" has a gematria, or numerical value, of sixty-one. What is rather intriguing about sixty-one is that after testing the research pattern used herein numerous times, it came to the writer's mind to add up the sum of the numbers involved in the pattern of seven specific occurrences that relate to the divine perspective. This pattern is the mainstay of understanding God's view of His text. The sum of the numbers of this set pattern of selected occurrences is equal to sixty-one. That sum is the same as the gematria, or numerical value of "I" or *ani*. Thus *ani*, I, is numerically connected to the set of occurrences that clarify the Creator's perspective on any Torah related matter.

"I" Ani, **אֲנִי**

א- 1, **נ** - 50, **י** - 10 = 61

The gematria value of "ani" = 61

The Pattern Of Occurrences

The first Occurrence	1
The Third Occurrence	3
The Seventh Occurrence	7
The Ninth Occurrence	9
The Tenth Occurrence	10
The Thirteenth Occurrence	13
The Eighteenth Occurrence	<u>18</u>
Sum Total	61

CHAPTER SIX

What Is a Torah Vessel?

A Torah Vessel

Concerning the numerical structure of the Torah, a Torah vessel is simply a Torah verse. It does not matter whether the verse is only a phrase, a sentence, or several sentences; a Torah vessel is a Torah verse. Again, this is one of those incidents where the author's use of a word may be perplexing to the uninformed reader. A vessel is a container; however, to this writer, a vessel is both a container and a vehicle of knowledge. This writer comes from a maritime background, historically, geographically, and vocationally.

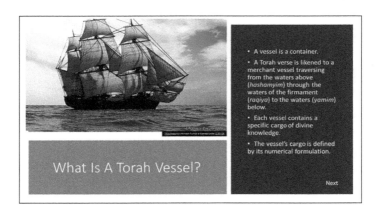

What Is A Torah Vessel?

- A vessel is a container.
- A Torah verse is likened to a merchant vessel traversing from the waters above (*hashamyim*) through the waters of the firmament (*raqiya*) to the waters (*yamim*) below.
- Each vessel contains a specific cargo of divine knowledge.
- The vessel's cargo is defined by its numerical formulation.

Next

Perhaps, the Creator uses what He has on hand to work with, or maybe it is of divine design. In any case, this has become the model and a good one at that. Throughout all this writer's discussion of the numerical structure of the Torah, a Torah verse shall be referred to as a sailing vessel commissioned in the waters above (heavens) and navigating the firmament to the seas of the earth. Each vessel has a specific numerical cargo, and the formulation of that cargo forms a numerical structure that relays divine instructions to the reader. By this writer's reckoning, there are 5,846 vessels of knowledge in the Torah, and each one of those vessels has been counted three times and cataloged in a database. That was a formidable and rewarding task that validated the existence of an embedded numerical structure.

How Large Is the Fleet of Vessels?

According to this writer's reckoning, there are 5,846 Torah vessels (verses). The size of the fleet of vessels is comprised of four math facts; four according to the numerical structure of the Torah relates to action. The Torah is indeed a book of the recorded acts of both the Creator and man.

5,846 VESSELS

5	*Heb* **Respect:** Five according to the numerical structure of the Torah, relates to honor and respect for one's creators, parents, coupled with a long life. The Creator is our third parent; if that concept appears to be a stretch for you, follow the context of the vessel. Which one of your two physical parents can guarantee you a long life?

8

Chet **Exchange:** Eight according to the numerical structure of the Torah relates to an exchange, either good or bad. The Torah is an exchange of the Creator's words of life given to man to bring life. Man, already has physical life; therefore, one should ask what manner of life is being addressed?

4

Dahlet **Action:** Four relates to action on the part of the Creator, man, or both. The Torah is an account of the actions of both from cover to cover.

6

Vav **Man:** Six relates to mankind or human nature. There is only one species of created beings to whom the oral and written aspects of the Torah might directly benefit.

The combined meaning of these four numerical facts is concerned with an exchange, which is founded on mutual respect and action, which ultimately is designed to benefit man. This exchange is intended to commence in respect and conclude with respect.

The Name of the Fleet Is "Torah."

Everything related to Torah has a purpose, and the whole of the Torah has a divine purpose for man. Unlike the animal kingdom whose instincts are genetically transmitted one to the next generation, the Torah is transferred orally; even when one silently reads the Torah, he hears his voice vocalizing the Torah internally.

> *This Book of the Torah shall not depart from your mouth; but you shall meditate on it day and night, that you may observe to do according to all that is written on it; for then you shall make your way prosperous, and then you shall have good success: (Joshua 1:8)*

Torah, תורה

According to Its Ordinals

<table>
<tr><td>ת = 22</td><td>Tav Command, Test, Division: Twenty-two according to the numerical structure of the Torah relates to:</td></tr>
</table>

The first ten (10)	A Command
The second ten (10)	A Test of a Command
The two (2)	Division, Separation, or Two Aspects of a Matter

The Hebrew word, Torah, is founded on three numerical facts (10 – 10 – 2), and the three numerical facts relate to an encounter with the Creator.

There Is a Primal Command

The primal foundational numeral, the first ten (10), is related to a command. The issue in the garden of Eden was theft in paradise, combined with ignoring the authority of the Creator. The flashpoints of the great flood were robbery and rebellion. Men chose to reject the commands of the Creator, albeit this time outside of the garden.

There Is a Test of That Primal Command

The secondary numeral, the second ten (10), is related to a test of a command. The issue is always theft, and since the garden event, theft has steadily plagued the world. Why is the issue theft? One of the first strong attachments in early childhood is the sense of mine; as a child progresses, he must learn the difference between mine and yours. If someone takes what belongs to him, he does not need someone to define his loss. In most cases, he knows that it is wrong to take what belongs to another unless the society surrounding him has taught him otherwise. Human beings are wired to understand that theft is wrong even though they participate in such behavior.

The third command of the Ten Words of the Covenant is, "you shall not take the name of the Lord, your God in vain." Three or third is related to an encounter with the Creator. Every person who has ever walked or shall walk upon this planet experiences an encounter with the Creator. That experience is related to the connection between vain and theft. Concerning the word vain, it means to consider something as empty, void, or meaningless. Many people in all cultures consider the teachings of the Creator as empty, void, or insignificant. The entire entity of creation belongs to the Creator, even our lowly selves. Mankind was created to serve their Creator, but the rebellious see it otherwise. Well, what has that to do with theft?

The Ten Words of the Covenant were written on two tablets of stone, five on the right and five on the left. These two tablets mirror one another.

I am the Lord Your God	You shall not kill
Make no graven images	You shall not commit adultery
Do not take "God" in vain	You shall not steal
Keep the Sabbath	You shall not bear false witness
Honor parents	You shall not covet

The core commandments are considering the Creator as empty, void, or meaningless. Some might be inclined to say that the commandment refers to cursing or using the Creator's name profanely. However, the being of the Creator cannot be separated from His name; He is His name. When His commands are treated as meaningless, His name is taken in vain. Notice that the parallel or mirror commandment is you shall not steal. When one denies the counsel of the Creator and considers His instructions as meaningless, he, in effect, takes from the Creator and becomes a thief in the Creator's world.

Some might be inclined to argue that the ten words of the covenant were meant only for the nation of Israel, but that is a misunderstanding. Israel is the firstborn nation of the nations, and they are destined to instruct all the other nations concerning the Torah. However, they are currently unable to adequately fill this destiny because they are a nation in exile. They are plagued with Torah rejecters. Note also that neither the Jews nor Judaism is the whole nation of Israel. The whole of Israel is dispersed among the nations.

> *And it shall come to pass, that every new moon, and every sabbath, shall all flesh come to worship before me, says the Lord:* (Isaiah 66:23)

Christians observe Sunday, Muslims observe Friday, but the prophet Isaiah says that the whole earth shall keep the Sabbath. Why will that be so? Because the Sabbath is the sign of the covenant. If one rejects the Sabbath, it is considered a rejection of the covenant, and that covenant is meant for the whole world. The entire world is our Father's, all of it.

> *It is a sign between me and the people of Israel forever; for in six days the Lord made heaven and earth, and on the seventh day he rested, and was refreshed:* (Shemot [Ex.] 31:17)

One might still be inclined to say that the Sabbath is the sign of the covenant with Israel and not the other nations. However, if that is the case, then why did the prophet Isaiah say that the whole of the earth would come and worship on the new moon and the Sabbath? The obvious answer is that all the nations shall embrace the covenant, of which the Sabbath is a sign. The nations are going to recognize that the Creator brought Israel out of Egypt. They shall no longer worship other gods, nor shall they take him in vain; no longer shall they labor on the Sabbath but shall honor and respect their three parents; no longer shall they commit murder, or practice adultery. They shall give only a true testimony, and they shall no longer permit themselves to entertain a strong desire of that which belongs to another. The whole of all of that is what the prophet Isaiah is referring to concerning worship on the Sabbath.

There Is a Division or Separation Resulting from That Primal Command

Finally, the third numeral fact, two (2), is related to division, separation, or two aspects of a matter. Since the days of the great flood, the three extended families of Shem, Cham, and Japheth have distanced themselves farther and farther from the Creator. The chronological progression of the faith and actions of Abraham, Isaac, and Jacob turned the flooding tide of rebellion and paved the way for the Sinai experience. The Torah presented on Mount Sinai is meant for all the world. The Sinai commands can be kept anywhere in the world.

Many in the world today take these commands in vain, considering them as meaningless to themselves. But, listen carefully to that third command, which represents an encounter with the Creator:

> You shall not take the name of the Lord your God in **vain**; for the Lord will not hold him **guiltless** who takes his name in **vain**:

As one can see, this is not a trivial matter in the eyes of the Creator, and it should not be a small matter in the minds of humankind, but unfortunately, it generally is.

⎢ = 6	*Vav* **Man:** Six relates to mankind or human nature. There is only one species of created beings to whom the oral and written aspects of the Torah might directly benefit.

Resh **Command, Test:** Twenty according to the numerical structure of the Torah relates to:

The first ten (10)	A Command
The second ten (10)	A Test of a Command

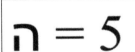

Heh **Five:** Five relates to honor and respect for one's creators, parents, coupled with a long life. The Creator is our third parent; if that concept appears to be a stretch for you, follow the context of the vessel. Which one of your two physical parents can guarantee you a long life?

49

What Types are the Two Types of Torah Vessels?

There are two types of Torah vessels. The first is absolute, meaning that it is absolute in the sense that it stands as it was first written and has not been modified for further clarification. The second is modified, meaning that the original draft of the vessel has been modified to expand the context of the original meaning to clarify the Creator's perspective on the initial draft of the vessel.

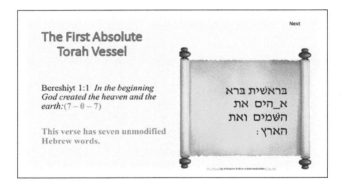

An Absolute Torah Vessel

Bereshiyt (Gn. 1:1) is the first example of an absolute vessel in the Torah. It is absolute because there are no *maqaphim* present in the text. An absolute vessel is sufficiently expressed from the outset to convey the Creator's perspective on the matter.

A modified Torah Vessel

Bereshiyt (Gn. 1:2) is the first example of a modified vessel in the Torah. It is changed because there are two *maqaphim* present in the text. The two *maqaphim* represent further clarification on the part of the Creator concerning the specific areas of His concern. Thus, two divine modifications have been made to this vessel.

What Is the Significance of These Two Types of Torah Vessels?

The first significance is that these two types of verses are strikingly different. They are purposefully made to be altered utilizing *maqaphim*. Approximately eighty-three percent of the 5,846 Torah vessels have been modified, and these modifications are accomplished through the insertion of over 11,400 *maqaphim*. It is inconceivable that the rules of Hebrew grammar would necessitate such excessive behavior.

The second significance is that the insertion of a *maqaph* into a Torah vessel alters the Hebrew word count, because words that are joined with a *maqaph*, or multiple *maqaphim*, become one word.

Every Torah vessel has a vessel formulation, whether it is absolute or modified. Thus, vessel one above has a formulation of (7-0-7), and vessel two has a formulation of (14-2-12). Therefore, the third significance is that all the vessels that have the same formulation, compare favorably with the fixed numerical principles which are related to those formulations.

The fourth significance is that these 5,846 witnesses affirm the validity of the numerical structure of the Torah. Five thousand, eight hundred and forty-six harmonious testimonies should convince most jurors of the presence of the numerical principles.

CHAPTER SEVEN

What Is an Absolute (Unmodified) Torah Vessel?

An Absolute Vessel Has Not Been Altered by The Creator

Again, a vessel is determined to be absolute because there are no *maqaphim* present in the text. An absolute vessel has enough information from the outset to convey the Creator's perspective on the matter.

How Many Absolute Vessels Are in The Torah?

According to this researcher's reckoning, there are one thousand eighteen (1,018) absolute vessels in the Torah, which comprise about seventeen percent of the Torah vessels.

What Is the Purpose of an Absolute Vessel?

An absolute vessel helps to clarify and validate each of the numerical principles related to the structure of the Torah. The first occurrence of an absolute vessel should be considered as the foundational platform for all the similar absolute vessels.

For clarity, the ten basic numerical principles were uncovered utilizing other strategies. The absolute vessels serve to validate the findings of the different approaches.

Some Absolute Facts

1 – 0 – 1

There are no absolute Torah vessels that have one word, and perhaps that is because nothing can be compared with the Creator, who is one.

2 – 0 – 2

There are no absolute Torah vessels that have two words, and perhaps that is because the matter of the Creator is one, and it cannot be divided, only the products of His creations can be divided.

3 – 0 – 3

The first vessel of thirteen vessels to contain three unmodified Hebrew words is *Bereshiyt 25:14. And Mishma, and Dumah, and Massa:* Apparently, these three men must have had a divine encounter with the Creator, and one should investigate this vessel from that perspective.

4 – 0 – 4

The first vessel of thirty-seven vessels to contain four unmodified Hebrew words is *Bereshiyt 21:24 And Abraham said, I will swear:* Four is related to action, and this is action on the part of the man, Abraham.

5 – 0 – 5

The first vessel of sixty-eight vessels to contain five unmodified Hebrew words is *Bereshiyt 6:8. And Noah found grace in the eyes of the Lord:*

Five is related to honor, respect, and a long life in the land, the whole of which, Noach experienced.

6 – 0 - 6

The first vessel of one hundred twenty-four vessels to contain six unmodified Hebrew words is *Bereshiyt* 9:20. *And Noah began to be a farmer, and he planted a vineyard:*

Six is related to mankind or human nature.

7 – 0 - 7

The first vessel of ninety-eight vessels to contain seven unmodified Hebrew words is *Bereshiyt* 1:1. *In the beginning God created the heaven and the earth:*

Seven is related to completion, cycle, or a cycle of repeated events, and the connection here is evident without elaboration.

8 – 0 - 8

The first vessel of eighty-eight vessels to contain eight unmodified Hebrew words is *Bereshiyt* 2:12. *And the gold of that land is good; there is bdellium and the onyx stone:*

These precious commodities were meant to be an exchange for man's obedience in the Garden of Eden; however, Adam and his wife failed their test and lost these precious gifts.

9 – 0 - 9

The first vessel of one hundred twenty-one vessels to contain nine, unmodified Hebrew words is *Bereshiyt* 4:3. *And in process of time it came to pass, that Cain brought of the fruit of the ground an offering to the Lord:*

Nine is related to a good or functional matter, something functioning according to the divine plan. The Creator considered Cain's action of bringing an offering as a good and functional matter.

10 – 0 - 10

The first vessel of one eighty-two vessels to contain ten unmodified Hebrew words is *Bereshiyt* 18:11. *Now Abraham and Sarah were old and well advanced in age; and it had ceased to be with Sarah after the manner of women:*

Ten is related to a command, covenant, or a test, and this test is associated with the overwhelming improbability of the command/covenant that Sarah would bear a child to Abraham.

There Are Twenty Absolute Vessel Formulations in The Torah.

While there are twenty absolute vessel formulations in the Torah, the lowest vessel formulation begins with (3-0-3) and the highest is (25-0-25). Five vessel formulations are lacking: (1-0-1), (2-0-2), (22-0-22) , (23-0-23) , and (24-0-24). The significance of the twenty absolute vessel formulations shall be discussed in chapter 10.

Chapter Eight

What Is a Modified Torah Vessel?

A Modified Vessel Has One or More Maqaphim

For our discussion, concerning the numerical structure of the Torah, a Hebrew *maqaph* is visually comparable to an English hyphen; however, its usage throughout the Torah seems to suggest a far more prominent role.

A Modified Vessel Has Three Components

A modified vessel has three significant components. The first being its original composition, the second being the number of critical modifications that were made to the vessel utilizing *maqaphim* inserted within the text. The third component is the final exhaustive composition.

The following graphic illustration is a random example depicting how to identify the location of *maqaphim* and the effects which they set in motion.

A RANDOM MODIFIED TORAH VESSEL

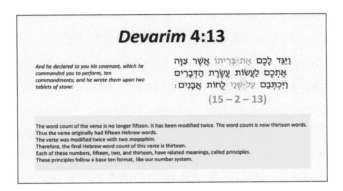

The next graphic illustration presents that information concerning the numerical structure of the Torah, which functions as a structural outline. That outline can also be likened to a roadmap to guide the reader along the path of understanding.

THE NUMERICAL STRUCTURE OF THIS MODIFIED VESSEL

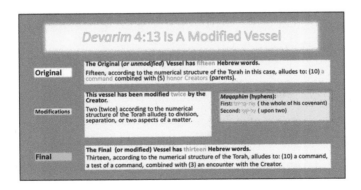

The intended purpose of all this numerical data is to convey the divine perspective more clearly to the seeking reader. This newfound information is like a personal and intimate conversation with the author of the Torah. It is neither forbidden to any person, nor is it beyond the capabilities of any reader. It is, however, only available to those who seek him.

In the next graphic illustration, this vessel shall be examined in the light of its embedded numerical structure. The initial context of this vessel is numerically expressed by the original text of fifteen Hebrew words. Ten relates to the command, and five relates to honor and respect for one's parents. Therefore, the foundational context is a father's command to his children. It is meant to be a situation of mutual family respect. Many find it difficult or unusual to depict the Creator as a loving Father, but that is what He is. The fifth commandment which parallels the fifth numerical principle is about honor or respect for one's parents.

THE FIFTH COMMANDMENT

> *Honor your father and your mother; that your days may be long upon the land which the Lord your God gives you: Shemot 20:12*

Any human parent cannot fulfill the promise that is attached to this commandment; only a divine parent, the Creator, can bring this promise to fulfillment. The Creator is our third parent.

Our Father is referring to the whole of the ten commands. Some may question the translation of the word, *aleph tav* (אֵת) since most Hebrew grammarians refer to it as a direct object indicator. *Aleph tav* meets all the criteria of a word, as far as the numerical structure of the Torah is concerned. *Aleph* is the ordinal one, and *tav* is the ordinal twenty-two; the sum of their ordinal values is twenty-three, and twenty-three relates to (10) command; combined with another (10) test of a command; combined with (3) an encounter with the Creator. That is the whole of the covenant.

Our Father modified the vessel twice with two *maqaphim*, to let us know that this covenant is divided into two aspects, one aspect on one tablet and the other aspect on the other tablet.

The final version of the vessel is comprised of thirteen Hebrew words. The ten words of the covenant are found twice in the Torah, and in both cases, they each contain thirteen vessels, meaning a command (10) and an encounter with the Creator (3).

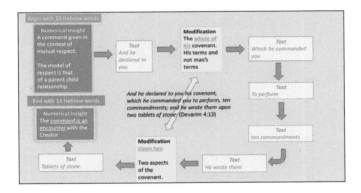

Original Composition

The original composition refers to the Hebrew word count before any modifications were made. In the above vessel (Devarim 4:13), the original piece contains fifteen Hebrew words.

Critical Modifications

There were two crucial modifications made by inserting two *maqaphim* in strategic locations. Those strategic placements are intended to expand the vessel's context in line with the Creator's perspective.

Final Exhaustive Composition

The final composition of the above vessel contains eleven non-compound Hebrew words, and two compound Hebrew words; creating a concluding Hebrew word count of thirteen. A compound word according to the numerical structure's usage is two or more Hebrew words that are joined with a *maqaph* to become one Hebrew word.

CHAPTER NINE

What Is a Vessel's Formulation?

What Is a Vessel's Formulation?

All 5,846 vessels in the Torah have a vessel formulation. Many vessels have the same three number formulation, and the vessels which have the same formulation will all have a meaningful relationship with one another. The graphic illustration below describes how to determine a vessel's formulation. When the vessel's classification is established, it is expressed as an array of numbers in parentheses separated by hyphens (3-0-3).

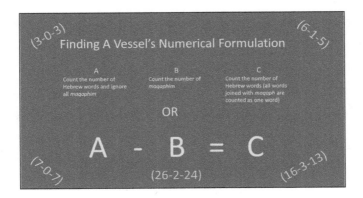

What Is the Significance of a Vessel's Formulation?

The primary significance of these specific vessel formulations is that like formulations have a similar pattern of meaning throughout the Torah. The consistent parallel relationship between numbers and meaning bears witness of the existence of a numerical structure embedded throughout the Torah text.

The other significance of these formulations is their proliferation throughout the Torah text, which leads one to ask, why are they there; what is their purpose, and most of all, who put them there? As a researcher, the task at hand is to observe any consistent patterns of behavior. Are there set principles involved in these phenomena? There are 5,846 vessels of Torah knowledge, which testify of a unique design of action; they establish a set pattern of principles; from that point on, one can only theorize concerning their origin and meaning.

When this pattern of numerical phenomena appears in multiple other applications throughout the Torah, it evidences an intricate unified design. Findings related to the alphabet, consonant clusters, words, vessels, chapters, books, and on and on; make it is increasingly difficult to understand how multiple authors, over scores of centuries, could have ever accomplished such complexity. In this writer's opinion, the numerical structure of the Torah is the signature of the Creator.

Thus, the modern scientific conception that the Torah is a divinely inspired document that is merely a cloud of foolishness. The significance of these 5,846 witnesses is of epic proportions. The structure is too complicated to have been engineered over centuries by the minds of men.

CHAPTER TEN

What Are the Twenty Absolute Vessel Formulations?

The Twenty Absolute Vessel Formulations

(1)	3-0-3	Thirteen occurrences are found in the Torah
(2)	4-0-4	Thirty-seven occurrences are found in the Torah
(3)	5-0-5	Sixty-eight occurrences are found in the Torah
(4)	6-0-6	One hundred twenty-four occurrences are found in the Torah.
(5)	7-0-7	Ninety-eight occurrences are found in the Torah.
(6)	8-0-8	Eighty-eight occurrences are found in the Torah.
(7)	9-0-9	One hundred twenty-one occurrences are found in the Torah.
(8)	10-0-10	Eighty-two occurrences are found in the Torah.
(9)	11-0-11	Eighty-eight occurrences are found in the Torah.
(10)	12-0-12	Seventy-eight occurrences are found in the Torah.
(11)	13-0-13	Sixty-four occurrences are found in the Torah.
(12)	14-0-14	Forty-nine occurrences are found in the Torah.
(13)	15-0-15	Thirty-two occurrences are found in the Torah.

(14)	16-0-16	Twenty-eight occurrences are found in the Torah.
(15)	17-0-17	Twenty-one occurrences are found in the Torah.
(16)	18-0-18	Fifteen occurrences are found in the Torah.
(17)	19-0-19	Three occurrences are found in the Torah.
(18)	20-0-20	Six occurrences are found in the Torah.
(19)	21-0-21	Two occurrences are found in the Torah.
(20)	22-0-22	none found
(21)	23-0-23	none found
(22)	24-0-24	none found
(23)	25-0-25	One occurrence is found in the Torah.

What Is the Significance of These Twenty Absolute Torah Vessels?

Twenty according to the numerical structure of the Torah is related to: (the first 10) a command; combined with (the second 10) a test of the command. The first of the six vessels to have the formulation (20-0-20) was a divine confirmation of the blessing that Isaac had bestowed upon Jacob.

> *Bereshiyt (Gn.) 28: 13. And, behold, the Lord stood above it, and said, I am the Lord God of Abraham your father, and the God of Isaac; the land on which you lie, to you will I give it, and to your seed:* **(20-0-20)**

Jacob was about to leave the land of Canaan, which his father Isaac had told him would be his inheritance according to the blessing of Isaac's father, Abraham. In this vessel, the Creator is affirming that promise to Jacob. If Jacob continued to listen to the Creator will be with him throughout his journeying outside of the land of promise (Bereshiyt 28:10-15).

What Is the Significance of The Eighteenth Formulation?

The formulation (20-0-20) is the eighteenth type of formulation in the list of the twenty absolute formulations. Eighteen is often associated with life since the consonants *chet* (ח) and *yud* (י) which spell the Hebrew word for life, *chai* (חי) have an ordinal numerical value of eighteen. The highest form of created life on the planet is man, and according to the numerical structure of the Torah, the ordinal number six is related to man. It is man who has received the bulk of the commands, and surely the whole of the written commands. Also, it is man who is responsible for listening and doing those commands. And man shall be tested according to those commands. There are six vessels with the (20-0-20) formulation in the Torah, and six according to the numerical structure of the Torah is related to man.

The Significance of Comparative Analysis

All 5,846 vessel formulations are in a database program, through which, the researcher can search and retrieve all the vessels which have any common number facts in their formulation. The database allows the vessel data to be both compared, contrasted, and evaluated according to scientific methods. Hopefully, this writer can, in the future, make a read-only, searchable database file available at a reasonable cost. Or perhaps, even a more sophisticated database program combined with the translated text shall be developed by others.

The Significance of Numerical Structure Validation

The twenty absolute vessel formulations validate the existence and relevance of the numerical principles. They are, however, not the only source of validation, but they do constitute over one thousand verifiable witnesses confirming the numerical structure of the Torah.

CHAPTER ELEVEN

What Is the Divine Perspective on Each Absolute Vessel Formulation?

What Is the Divine Perspective on Each Absolute Formulation?

T he divine perspective was covered in chapter 5, in case you require a quick review. Insights into the divine perspective on any Torah matter can be investigated by examining a specific pattern of seven occurrences of a Torah matter. The graphic illustration below is the format for this divine pattern.

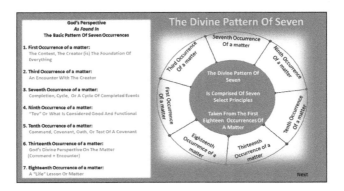

The Divine Perspective on the Absolute Vessel Formulation 1-0-1

The Creator is "one," therefore, nothing can be compared with the Creator. There are not any vessels with an absolute formulation of (1-0-1), nor are there any vessels that end with one word after being modified.

The Divine Perspective on the Absolute Vessel Formulation 2-0-2

For reasons that are yet to be determined, there are no vessels with an absolute formulation of (2-0-2); however, there are two vessels in the Torah that have a final word count of two Hebrew words.

This vessel is one of those hidden treasures that overwhelm one when they are uncovered by the numerical structure of the Torah. Thirteen (13), according to the numerical structure is related to: (10) a command combined with (3) and encounter with the Creator. One of the unique characteristics of the Torah is that the doubling of words or concepts. That linguistic mechanism is used to emphasize the absoluteness of that word or concept. This vessel is the thirteenth vessel in the thirteenth chapter. The two thirteens are strategic numerical markers.

The Divine Perspective on the Absolute Vessel Formulation 3-0-3
The Keyword Is Encounter

First Occurrence: The Creator (is) The Foundation of Everything

Ber. 25:14. *And Mishma, and Dumah, and Massa:*

Third Occurrence: An Encounter with The Creator

Ber. 43:1 *And the famine was severe in the land:*

Seventh Occurrence: Completion, Cycle, or a Cycle of Repeated Events

She. 28:13 *And you shall make fixtures of gold:*

Ninth Occurrence: A Good Matter, Functioning According to The Divine Plan

VaY. 14:56 *And for a swelling, and for a scab, and for a bright spot:*

Tenth Occurrence: Command, Covenant, Oath, or Test of a Covenant

BeM. 6:24 *The Lord bless you, and keep you:*

Thirteenth Occurrence: Command, Covenant, Oath, or Test of a Covenant; combined with *An Encounter With The Creator*

Dev. 28:17 *Cursed shall be your basket and your store:*

Eighteenth Occurrence: Command, Covenant, Oath, or Test of a Covenant; combined with *An Exchange (Good or Bad)*

Not available

The Divine Perspective on the Absolute Vessel Formulation 4-0-4 The Keyword Is Action

First Occurrence: The Creator (is) The Foundation of Everything

Ber. 21:24 *And Abraham said, I will swear:*

Third Occurrence: An Encounter with The Creator

Ber. 24:34 *And he said, I am Abraham's servant:*

Seventh Occurrence: Completion, Cycle, or a Cycle of Repeated Events

She. 1:4 *Dan, and Naphtali, Gad, and Asher:*

Ninth Occurrence: A Good Matter, Functioning According to The Divine Plan

She. 15:18 *The Lord shall reign forever and ever:*

Tenth Occurrence: Command, Covenant, Oath, or Test of a Covenant

She. 16:30 *So the people rested on the seventh day:*

Thirteenth Occurrence: Command, Covenant, Oath, or Test of a Covenant; combined with An Encounter with The Creator

She. 25:34 *And its tongs, and its trays, shall be of pure gold:*

Eighteenth Occurrence: Command, Covenant, Oath, or Test of a Covenant; combined with An Exchange (Good or Bad)

BeM. 21:31 *Thus Israel lived in the land of the Amorites:*

The Divine Perspective on the Absolute Vessel Formulation 5-0-5
The Keyword Is Respect

First Occurrence: The Creator (is) The Foundation of Everything

Ber. 6:8 *And Noah found grace in the eyes of the Lord:*

Third Occurrence: An Encounter with The Creator

Ber. 12:9 *And Abram journeyed, going on still toward the Negev:*

Seventh Occurrence: Completion, Cycle, or a Cycle of Repeated Events

Ber. 26:35 *And they made life bitter for Isaac and for Rebekah:*

Ninth Occurrence: A Good Matter, Functioning According to The Divine Plan

Ber. 30:28. *And he said, Appoint me your wages, and I will give it:*

Tenth Occurrence: Command, Covenant, Oath, or Test of a Covenant

Ber. 31:24. *And Jacob took a stone, and set it up for a pillar:*

Thirteenth Occurrence: Command, Covenant, Oath, or Test of a Covenant; combined with An Encounter With The Creator

Ber. 36:1 *Now these are the generations of Esau, who is Edom:*

Eighteenth Occurrence: Command, Covenant, Oath, or Test of a Covenant; combined with An Exchange (Good or Bad)

She, 6:21. *And the sons of Izhar; Korah, and Nepheg, and Zichri:*

The Divine Perspective on the Absolute Vessel Formulation 6-0-6
The Keyword Is Man

First Occurrence: The Creator (is) The Foundation of Everything

> Ber. 9:20. *And Noah began to be a farmer, and he planted a vineyard:*

Third Occurrence: An Encounter with The Creator

> Ber. 10:6. *And the sons of Ham; Kush, and Egypt, and Put, and Canaan:*

Seventh Occurrence: Completion, Cycle, or a Cycle of Repeated Events

> Ber. 13:13. *But the men of Sodom were exceedingly wicked and sinners before the Lord:*

This vessel is one of those hidden treasures that simply overwhelm one, when they are uncovered by the numerical structure of the Torah. Thirteen (13) according to the numerical structure is related to: (10) a command combined with (3) and encounter with the Creator. One of the unique characteristics of the Torah is that the doubling of words or concepts is used to emphasize the absoluteness of that word or concept. This vessel is the thirteenth vessel in the thirteenth chapter. The two thirteens are strategic numerical markers.

Ninth Occurrence: A Good Matter, Functioning According to The Divine Plan

Ber. 21:34. *And Abraham sojourned in the Philistines' land many days:*

Tenth Occurrence: Command, Covenant, Oath, or Test of a Covenant

Ber. 25:1. *Then again Abraham took a wife, and her name was Keturah:*

Thirteenth Occurrence: Command, Covenant, Oath, or Test of a Covenant; combined with An Encounter With The Creator

Ber. 28:10. *And Jacob went out from Beersheba, and went toward Haran:*

Eighteenth Occurrence: Command, Covenant, Oath, or Test of a Covenant; combined with An Exchange (Good or Bad)

Ber. 36:36. *And Hadad died, and Samlah of Masrekah reigned in his place:*

The Divine Perspective on the Absolute Vessel Formulation 7-0-7
The Keyword Is Completion

First Occurrence: The Creator (is) The Foundation of Everything

Ber. 1:1. *In the beginning God created the heaven and the earth:*

Third Occurrence: An Encounter with The Creator

Ber. 6:11. *The earth also was corrupt before God, and the earth was filled with violence:*

Seventh Occurrence: Completion, Cycle, or a Cycle of Repeated Events

Ber. 15:8. *And he said, Lord God, how shall I know that I shall inherit it:*

Ninth Occurrence: A Good Matter, Functioning According to The Divine Plan

Ber. 17:26. *In the same day was Abraham circumcised, and Ishmael his son:*

Tenth Occurrence: Command, Covenant, Oath, or Test of a Covenant

Ber. 19:6. *And Lot went out the door to them, and closed the door after him:*

Thirteenth Occurrence: Command, Covenant, Oath, or Test of a Covenant; combined with An Encounter with The Creator

Ber. 30:12. *And Zilpah Leah's maid bore Jacob a second son:*

Eighteenth Occurrence: Command, Covenant, Oath, or Test of a Covenant; combined with An Exchange (Good or Bad)

Ber. 36:26. *And these are the children of Dishon; Hemdan, and Eshban, and Ithran, and Keran:*

The Divine Perspective on the Absolute Vessel Formulation 8-0-8
The Keyword Is Exchange

First Occurrence: The Creator (is) The Foundation of Everything

> Ber. 2:12. *And the gold of that land is good; there is bdellium and the onyx stone:*

Third Occurrence: An Encounter with The Creator

> Ber. 7:20. *Fifteen cubits upward did the waters prevail; and the mountains were covered:*

Seventh Occurrence: Completion, Cycle, or a Cycle of Repeated Events

> Ber. 17:2. *And I will make my covenant between me and you, and will multiply you exceedingly:*

Ninth Occurrence: A Good Matter, Functioning According to The Divine Plan

> Ber. 18:9. *And they said to him, Where is Sarah your wife? And he said, Behold, in the tent:*

Tenth Occurrence: Command, Covenant, Oath, or Test of a Covenant

> Ber. 18:17. *And the Lord said, Shall I hide from Abraham that thing which I do:*

Thirteenth Occurrence: Command, Covenant, Oath, or Test of a Covenant; combined with An Encounter With The Creator

Ber. 27:8. *Now therefore, my son, obey my voice according to that which I command you:*

Eighteenth Occurrence: Command, Covenant, Oath, or Test of a Covenant; combined with An Exchange (Good or Bad)

Ber. 35:19. *And Rachel died, and was buried in the way to Ephrath, which is Beth-Lehem:*

The Divine Perspective on the Absolute Vessel Formulation 9-0-9
The Keyword Is Functional

First Occurrence: The Creator (is) The Foundation of Everything

Ber. 4:3. *And in process of time it came to pass, that Cain brought of the fruit of the ground an offering to the Lord:*

Third Occurrence: An Encounter with The Creator

Ber. 9:26. *And he said, Blessed be the Lord God of Shem; and Canaan shall be his slave:*

Seventh Occurrence: Completion, Cycle, or a Cycle of Repeated Events

Ber. 11:2. *And it came to pass, as they journeyed from the east, that they found a plain in the land of Shinar; and they lived there:*

Ninth Occurrence: A Good Matter, Functioning According to The Divine Plan

Ber. 14:19. *And he blessed him, and said, Blessed be Abram of the most high God, possessor of heaven and earth:*

Tenth Occurrence: Command, Covenant, Oath, or Test of a Covenant

Ber. 17:6. *And I will make you exceedingly fruitful, and I will make nations of you, and kings shall come out of you:*

Thirteenth Occurrence: Command, Covenant, Oath, or Test of a Covenant; combined with An Encounter With The Creator

> Ber. 22:18. *And in your seed shall all the nations of the earth be blessed; because you have obeyed my voice:*

Eighteenth Occurrence: Command, Covenant, Oath, or Test of a Covenant; combined with An Exchange (Good or Bad)

> Ber. 29:16. *And Laban had two daughters; the name of the elder was Leah, and the name of the younger was Rachel:*

The Divine Perspective on the Absolute Vessel
Formulation 10-0-10
The Keyword Is Command

First Occurrence: The Creator (is) The Foundation of Everything

Ber. 18:11. *Now Abraham and Sarah were old and well advanced in age; and it had ceased to be with Sarah after the manner of women:*

Third Occurrence: An Encounter with The Creator

Ber. 18:22. *And the men turned their faces from there, and went toward Sodom; but Abraham still stood before the Lord:*

Seventh Occurrence: Completion, Cycle, or a Cycle of Repeated Events

Ber. 31:44. *Now therefore come, let us make a covenant, you and me; and let it be for a witness between me and you:*

Ninth Occurrence: A Good Matter, Functioning According to The Divine Plan

Ber. 36:21. *And Dishon, and Ezer, and Dishan; these are the chiefs of the Horites, the children of Seir in the land of Edom:*

Tenth Occurrence: Command, Covenant, Oath, or Test of a Covenant

Ber. 37:33. *And he knew it, and said, It is my son's coat; an evil beast has devoured him; Joseph is without doubt torn in pieces:*

Thirteenth Occurrence: Command, Covenant, Oath, or Test of a Covenant; combined with An Encounter With The Creator

Ber. 40:18. *And Joseph answered and said, This is the interpretation; The three baskets are three days:*

Eighteenth Occurrence: Command, Covenant, Oath, or Test of a Covenant; combined with An Exchange (Good or Bad)

Ber. 46:2. *And God spoke to Israel in the visions of the night, and said, Jacob, Jacob; And he said, Here am I:*

Something Extraordinary, A Structure Within A Structure.

The numerical structure of the Torah can contain a structure within a structure. In the previous collection of absolute vessels having a formulation of (10-0-10), one might be puzzled with how Jacob's response to Joseph's bloody coat fits in with the principle word *command*.

First Occurrence in The Pattern of Seven: *The Creator (is) The Foundation of Everything*

> *First Occurrence: The Creator (is) The Foundation of Everything*
>> Ber. 18:11. *Now Abraham and Sarah were old and well advanced in age; and it had ceased to be with Sarah after the manner of women:* Pregnancy was beyond the capabilities of Abraham and Sarah.

Second Occurrence in The Pattern of Seven: *Division, Separation, or Two Aspects of a Matter*

> *Third Occurrence: An Encounter with The Creator*
>> Ber. 18:22. *And* the men turned their faces *from there, and went toward Sodom; but* Abraham still stood before the Lord:

Third Occurrence in The Pattern of Seven: *An Encounter with The Creator*

> *Seventh Occurrence: Completion, Cycle, or a Cycle of Repeated Events*
>> Ber. 31:44. *Now therefore come, let us make a covenant, you and me; and let it be for a* witness *between me and you:* The heap of stones was a reminder that the Creator was a witness to this event.

Fourth Occurrence in The Pattern of Seven: *Action on The Part of The Creator or Man*

> *Ninth Occurrence: A Good Matter, Functioning According to The Divine Plan*

Ber. 36:21. *And Dishon, and Ezer, and Dishan; these are the chiefs of the Horites, the children of Seir in the land of Edom:* These men are the leaders, or men of action.

Fifth Occurrence in The Pattern of Seven: *Honor Creators, Long Life in The Land*

Tenth Occurrence: *Command, Covenant, Oath, or Test of a Covenant*

Ber. 37:33. *And he knew it, and said, It is my son's coat; an evil beast has devoured him; Joseph is without doubt torn in pieces:* This event was a mental threat, and a test of the covenant between Jacob and the Creator, since apparently Joseph's life was cut short. Was the covenant being mutually respected?

Sixth Occurrence in The Pattern of Seven: *Related to Mankind or Human Nature*

Thirteenth Occurrence: *Command, Covenant, Oath, or Test of a Covenant; combined with An Encounter with The Creator*

Ber. 40:18. *And Joseph answered and said, This is the interpretation; The three baskets are three days:* This dream affected the lives of both the dreamer and the dream interpreter.

Seventh Occurrence in The Pattern of Seven: *Completion, Cycle, or a Cycle of Repeated Events*

Eighteenth Occurrence: *Command, Covenant, Oath, or Test of a Covenant; combined with An Exchange (Good or Bad)*

Ber. 46:2. *And God spoke to Israel in the visions of the night, and said, Jacob, Jacob; And he said, Here am I:* This method of communication was both a complete message and a continuous cycle of communications.

This example of a structure within a structure can be found within the divine pattern of seven occurrences in any correctly assembled research data. Again, it is another signature mark of the Creator. This number framework is our Father's Hebrew.

Why Does the List Commence with the 3-0-3 Formulation?

While one can only theorize concerning the questions of why, what does make sense according to the patterned usage is that the absolute formulations are as straight forward of as possible. Their assertions are none other than firsthand statements, as if we obtained them from the core of the Creator's thinking, constituting an intimate encounter with the Creator. The third numerical principal is an encounter with the Creator, and the doubled use of three in the formulation asserts the absoluteness of the matter.

There are only thirteen vessels with the formulation (3-0-3) in the whole of the Torah. From the *"Shema"* passage of the Torah (*Devarim* chapter 6), it is known that the Creator is "one" or "echad." Well, it just so happens that the word *"echad,"* which means one has an ordinal value of thirteen, therefore the concept of "one, *echad*" is numerically connected with thirteen. Perhaps, one might be permitted to say that the Creator is both one and thirteen.

Why Does the List Conclude with the 25-0-25 Formulation?

Twenty-five according to the numerical structure of the Torah relates to (the first ten) command, combined with (the second ten) a test of a command, and finally connected with (five) honor and respect for one's creators or parents. Bear in mind, of course, that the Creator is the first of our three parents or creators.

There is only one vessel in the whole of the Torah that has the vessel formulation of (25-0-25), and one according to the numerical structure of the Torah is related to the Creator, who is the foundation of everything. Perhaps, this is the *why* of these twenty absolute vessel formulations; they are links to the treasure that only the seekers shall find.

> *And you shall rejoice before the Lord your God, you, and your son, and your daughter, and your manservant, and your maidservant, and the Levite who is inside your gates, and the stranger, and the orphan, and the widow, who are among you, in the place which the Lord your God has chosen to place his name there: (Devarim 16:11) (25-0-25)*

Chapter Twelve

A Sequential Catalogue of the Twenty Absolute Vessel Formulations

A Sequential Catalogue of the Twenty Absolute Vessel Formulations

The entire categorizing and cataloging of the vessels of the Torah rested upon my labors. Chiefly, due to the is a lack of resources relative to the Hebrew *maqaphim* and their effects upon the text. It may take some time before others pick up the task and assemble this type of research into a software program. The best that I can presently provide for you, the serious student of Torah, is a chronological listing of the vessels related to each absolute formulation.

In the Appendix, all the absolute vessels are listed in chronological order for the reader's benefit. These absolute vessels provide over one thousand witnesses which testify of the presence of a numerical structure throughout the Torah.

They are organized into five columns as listed below:

Vessel:
refers to the vessel number or ordinal number verse in the Torah.

Book:
refers to the name of the book in the Torah.

Chp. :

refers to the chapter number in the book.

Vs. :

refers to the verse number in the chapter.

Form. :

refers to the vessel's numerical formulation.

Vessel Number	Book	Chp.	Vs.	Form.
673	Bereshiyt	25	14	3-0-3
699	Bereshiyt	26	6	3-0-3
1,292	Bereshiyt	43	1	3-0-3
1,492	Bereshiyt	49	18	3-0-3
1,536	Shemot	1	3	3-0-3
2,129	Shemot	22	17	3-0-3
2,304	Shemot	28	13	3-0-3
3,164	VaYikra	14	55	3-0-3
3,165	VaYikra	14	56	3-0-3
3,845	BeMidbar	6	24	3-0-3
4,495	BeMidbar	26	8	3-0-3
5,611	Devarim	28	5	3-0-3
5,623	Devarim	28	17	3-0-3

Some ~~Coincidental~~ Numerical Facts

The first absolute vessel formulation is three Hebrew words with zero modifications.

One or first is related to the Creator (is) the foundation.

Three or third is common to encountering the Creator; "*on the third day*" the people met the Creator on Mount Sinai.

There are thirteen vessels with the 3-0-3 formulation.

The commands given on Mount Sinai are expressed in thirteen vessels.

The second set of the ten words in Deuteronomy are expressed in thirteen vessels.

The Torah says that the Creator is one (*echad*). *Echad* has a numerical value of thirteen.

The core vessel of these thirteen vessels is Shemot (Ex. 28:13).

Hard Works Pays Great Benefits

It took this researcher several years of investigation and contemplation to come to the point of absolute confidence in the numerical structure. The consistent testimonies of these absolute vessels sealed my confidence so much that before turning to a commentary or lexicon about a Torah vessel, I must examine the numerical structure. It is like having access to the author's outline notes at your fingertips. Yes, it does take some hard work to master the basic skills, but the rewards are immense.

Some Closing Thoughts

According to my reckoning there are 1,018 absolute vessels, and every one of them has been listed above. These 1,018 vessels constitute over seventeen percent of the Torah text.

These vessels were included in this book to provide the reader with enough information that one can rest assured that enough research has been done to make a reasonable conclusion. Also, to provide the reader with a primary source to use in his initial investigations into the numerical structure of the Torah.

CHAPTER THIRTEEN

The Base Ten Numerical Structure Is A Divine Encounter

What Is the Base Ten Numerical Structure?

> ### The Decimal Numeral System
>
> (also called base-ten positional numeral system)
>
> Many numeral systems of ancient civilizations use ten and its powers for representing numbers, possibly because there are ten fingers on two hands and people started counting by using their fingers. Examples are Brahmi numerals, Greek numerals, Hebrew numerals, Roman numerals, and Chinese numerals. Very large numbers were difficult to represent in these old numeral systems, and only the best mathematicians were able to multiply or divide large numbers. These difficulties were completely solved with the introduction of the Hindu–Arabic numeral system for representing integers. This system has been extended to represent some non-integer numbers, called decimal fractions or decimal numbers for forming the decimal numeral system.
>
> https://en.wikipedia.org/wiki/Decimal

The number system employed in researching the numerical structure of the Torah is the decimal system (base ten), which is centered around units of ten. Perhaps, this is the fifth dimension of ten: (1) the ten principles, (2) ten sayings, (3) ten words, (4) ten tests. If it is the fifth, then it is related to honor and respect. Continuing with the same train of thought, the sixth dimension of ten might allude to the ten fingers and ten toes common to all humanity. Six or sixth is related to mankind or human nature.

The illustration at the right breaks down the number thirteen according to the base ten system. Thirteen is the same as one ten and three ones, or one unit of ten, and one partial group of ten having three ones.

Twenty-three is the same as two tens and three ones, or two units of ten, and one partial unit of ten having three ones.

Thirty-three is the same as Three tens and three ones, or three units of ten, and one partial unit of ten having three ones.

In the Torah, base ten research can be extended to whatever numerical quantity is required to cover the task.

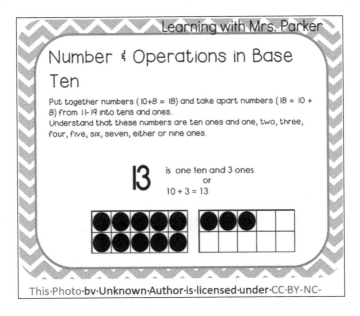

Connecting the Base Ten System to the Numerical Principles

As a result of years of research, the ten principles were developed by numerous applications of comparative analysis. However, that does not mean that they should not be further modified for clarification.

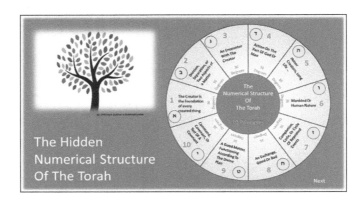

Defining Unit Ten in Repetitive Applications

There is a quirky problem that can arise when researching a matter according to the numerical structure, which is resolved with the aid of the base ten strategies. The problem lies in the multitude of data that might be encountered in a research sampling.

> Devarim 32:39. *See now that I am he, and there is no god with me; I kill, and I make alive; I wound, and I heal; nor is there any who can deliver out of my hand:*

An example may be found concerning the first name given for the Creator (Elohim), which is the name of his choosing. Elohim is in the plural format. The polytheists hover over it, the pious magnify it, and the scholars both secular and religious see-saw over its perplexities, but what is the Creator's perspective on the matter? Well, the words *"Elohim or elohim"* are found two hundred twenty-eight times in the Torah, and that translates to twenty-two units of ten and a partial group of eight ones. The last occurrence of Elohim, in the Torah, is the two hundred twenty-eighth occurrence, and it is found in *Devarim* 32:39. The Creator makes it clear that He alone is God, and that no person can deliver one out of His hand. No person, such as a god-man messiah, can deliver one out of his hand.

According to the numerical principles, the twenty-two units of ten would involve the tenth principle twenty-two times. The tenth principle is command, covenant, oath, a test of a command (or covenant). Notice that ten presently only has four defining terms, and the number 228 has twenty-two units of ten. How does one apply these defining terms in the other eighteen groups of ten, or for that matter, in the first four units of ten? Currently, the position taken is to consider the context and relate the terms appropriately. The background of this two hundred twenty-eighth occurrence of Elohim involves all four aspects of the tenth principle.

According to the numerical principles, the eight would involve the eighth principle: an exchange (good or bad).

	Context! Context! **Context!**	
	How Does One Apply The Tenth Principle?	The Solution Is Always Context
1st Ten	Command	The four options yield to context in every application.
2nd Ten	Covenant	
3rd Ten	Oath	
4th Ten	Test of command	Torah Hebrew is all about context!!!
5th Ten	???	
10th Ten	???	
50th Ten	???	
100th Ten	???	

The Creator is commanding one to see and understand that He alone is the seal of the oath and covenant, and that this statement is a test of one's respect concerning this command; secondly, there is nothing good nor bad with which he can be exchanged.

The Base Ten System Acknowledges A Divine Encounter

Additionally, the word Elohim was cataloged, according to the numerical structure to the thirty-fifth occurrence, for a study. What is significant is that each of the thirty-five incidents was meaningfully congruent with the numerical principles. For another study, the sacred name, Y-_-V-H (Lord), was cataloged to the one-hundredth occurrence, with each event maintaining a meaningful harmonious relationship with the numerical principles. This type of extensive research can be done with every word in the Torah, and it will yield meaningful cooperative relationships with the numerical principles. How could such a mathematical complexity have been the product of many men over a long time? The statistical probability of that accomplishment would be staggering. If the numerical relationship only applied to words, that alone would be a stellar accomplishment, but that is merely the launching pad for a galactic adventure of infinite numerical connections. The same numerical relationships are simultaneously maintained for every consonant, consonant cluster, along with many other linguistic Torah Hebrew mechanisms.

This overwhelming numerical complexity can allude to nothing other than an encounter with the Creator. Consider, is it remotely possible that a collection of men could accomplish such a task? If so, why has it never been brought to light? According to this researcher's knowledge, this depth of instruction concerning the numerical structure of the Torah has never been publicly published. Indeed, in the period of some thirty-five hundred years since the wilderness wanderings, someone would have hinted at the structure if it were man's doing.

Why now, one might ask? Two words come to mind in response to those two words; *technology* and *timing*. Without the aid of computer technology, such research would have been an arduous task. Now regarding timing, every generation has likened their times as nearing the end of the

Creator's patience. Perhaps, that end is near, or maybe the Creator has something special in mind. What is known is that the revelation of this structure is something historically special.

CHAPTER FOURTEEN

It Is a Matter of Divine Perspective and Purpose

Why Is Divine Perspective Listed First Before the Purpose?

He is the Creator, and we are the created; that alone should establish why the divine perspective should be listed first. However, in the reality of life, maintaining that prime perspective is kin to the art of juggling. Often the divine view is not in the grasp of one's hands.

The Divine Perspective

Mankind is the culminating factor of the whole of creation. The universe was created with the earth in mind, and the earth was created with humankind in mind, man was created with royalty in mind, and while that plan may seem to have gone awry due to man's insubordination, it has only been tempo-

rarily delayed. The Creator's perspective on the purpose of creation leads the way in the Torah, is clearly stated in the ninth saying of the ten sayings of creation, or the twenty-eighth vessel of the Torah.

> *Bereshiyt 1:28. And God blessed them, and God said to them, Be fruitful[1], and multiply[2], and replenish[3] the earth, and subdue[4] it; and have dominion[5] over the fish of the sea and the birds of the air, and over every living thing that moves upon the earth:*

The Twenty-Eighth Vessel of the Torah

Twenty-eight, according to the numerical structure of the Torah relates to:

[The first ten]	a divine command
[The second ten]	a test of the divine command
[The Eight]	an exchange, which in this case involves a long life

The Ninth Saying of the Ten Sayings of Creation

Nine or ninth is related to a good matter, something that is functioning according to the divine plan. From the Creator's perspective, if something is good, it is functional and will always produce a positive outcome. If it is not good, it is, therefore, evil or dysfunctional, and will always provide a negative result.

Mankind's First Commission Is a Package of Five Verbal Commands

Bereshiyt 1:28 is mankind's first command, which is also the Creator's purpose for mankind. His goal for man is a package of five verbal commands, and five is related to honor and respect for one's parents together with a long life. These five verbal commands also follow the numerical structure as follows:

[1] **First Principle:** Foundation, The Creator, is the foundation.

To be fruitful is the foundational purpose of man's existence. The modern-day obsession with alternative lifestyles and dysfunctional family units appears to run awry of the primal divine purpose for humanity.

[2] **Second Principle:** Division, Separation, or Two Aspects of a Matter

Cellular division if the core of the process of life from its commencement. To multiply involves propagation. Humanity was divinely commanded to propagate, yet many societies have adapted strategies to limit or curtail the multiplication of their populations.

[3] **Third Principle:** An Encounter with The Creator

This principle is the showdown; it is where the rubber meets the road. The concept of replenishment, in this case, infers the perpetuation of the above commands: be fruitful, multiply, what could be so difficult about that? However, replenishment should be linked with the continuation of the same qualities or standards as the original. In short, it means to maintain divine standards.

[4] Fourth Principle: Action on the Part of God or Man or Both

This fourth principle marks the action that man was designed and commanded to perform. The English translation employs the word subdue to convey the meaning of *kivshuha* (כִבְשֻׁהָ). The English essence of the verb subdue means to "overcome by force." There is a distinct air of militancy attached to the word subdue. How does a Hebrew reader respond to the word kivshuha (כִבְשֻׁהָ)?

Strong's Exhaustive Concordance כִבְשֻׁהָ

bring into bondage, force, keep under, subdue, bring into subjection

A primitive root; to tread down; hence, negatively, to disregard; positively, to conquer, subjugate, violate -- bring into bondage, force, keep under, subdue, bring into subjection.

Again, that sense of militancy is borne by its classical definition, but the most critical question to be asked is what did the author of the Torah have in mind when he employed this Hebrew term in the Torah? To answer that query, the strategy of the divine perspective mentioned in chapter 5, was utilized to obtain the seven specific occurrences of kivshuha (כִבְשֻׁהָ) as found in the Torah. However, there is a problem here; this word is only found this one time in the Torah. It cannot be compared with any other Torah vessel or word usage.

In that case, the first three-consonants form a cluster (כְבַשׁ) which can be researched since the three consonants comprise seventy-five of the whole word. In the formation of a Hebrew word, every consonant extends the meaning, thereby reflecting the divine nature of Torah Hebrew words.

The Hebrew word *kivshuha* (כְּבָשָׁה), which is translated "subdue," is only found one time in the Torah. Therefore, the comparative analysis must be related to the three-consonant cluster (כבש). An analysis of the first eighteen occurrences of these occurrences involves four word-concepts. It is often considered that one can be better known by the company one keeps. The company that these three consonants (כבש) keep in this sampling consists of four

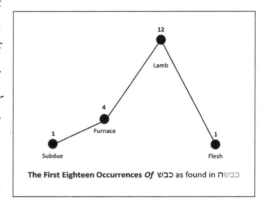

related words: subdue, furnace, lamb, and flesh. They are tallied as follows: subdue (1), furnace (4), lamb (12), flesh (1). Every word in this family of words has one common thematic connection; in other words, there is one common word-concept which can be associated with every one of them. That common word-concept is *witness*.

Only the first occurrence of these three consonants in this specific sampling of the eighteen first occurrences involves the English word *subdue*. That is fitting since that word is only found once in the Torah.

One must also take note of how this family of related words is found in the pattern of the divine perspective. Two times the consonants are connected to the word furnace, and four times they are connected to lambs. None of the six words are related to any manner of militancy. The four connections with lambs are anything but militant. What is going on here? Well, it is quite simple: the first connection is with the concept of subduing; however, the following six relationships are related to witnesses; the furnace is a witness of the presence of the Creator, and the lambs are witnesses before the Creator.

> ### A Summary of The Divine Perspective on "כבש"
> #### *A Pattern of Seven*
>
> **First:** *Foundation*
> Ber. 1:28. *And God blessed them, and God said to them, Be fruitful, and multiply, and replenish the earth, and* **subdue** *it: and have dominion over the fish of the sea, and over the birds of the air, and over every living thing that moves upon the earth.* **(22 - 3 - 19)**
>
> **Third:** *An Encounter*
> Ber. 21:28. *And Abraham set seven ewe* **lambs** *of the flock by themselves.* **(7 - 1 - 6)**
>
> **Seventh:** *Completion, Cycle*
> She. 9:8. *And the Lord said to Moses and to Aaron, Take handfuls of ashes from the* **furnace**, *and let Moses sprinkle it toward the heaven in the sight of Pharaoh.* **(17 - 2 - 15)**
>
> **Ninth:** *A Good Matter, Functioning According To Divine Plan*
> She. 12:5. *Your* **lamb** *shall be without blemish, a male of the first year; you shall take it out from the sheep, or from the goats.* **(12 - 3 - 9)**
>
> **Tenth:** *Command, Covenant, or Test*
> She. 19:18. *And Mount Sinai was altogether in smoke, because the Lord descended upon it in fire; and its smoke ascended as the smoke of a* **furnace**, *and the whole mount trembled greatly.* **(18 - 1 - 17)**
>
> **Thirteenth:** *Command or Test + A Divine Encounter*
> She. 29:39. *The one* **lamb** *you shall offer in the morning; and the other lamb you shall offer at evening.* **(11 - 1 - 10)**
>
> **Eighteenth:** *Command + An Exchange (A life Principle)*
> VaY. 12:6. *And when the days of her purifying are fulfilled, for a son, or for a daughter, she shall bring a* **lamb** *of the first year for a burnt offering, and a young pigeon, or a turtledove, for a sin offering, to the door of the Tent of Meeting, to the priest.* **(22 - 6 - 16)**

The dominant word-concept in the pattern of the divine perspective is *lamb,* and the first usage of lamb in the Torah is related to the concept of witnesses (*Bereshiyt* 21:28). Lambs are certainly not the type of animals that one would be inclined to associate with the idea of militancy.

[5] **Fifth Principle**: Honor, Respect for Parents, combined with a Long Life

This fifth verbal command concerning having dominion is related to the living creatures in the sea below, the land creatures, and the birds of the air. These creatures span the environs of earth. This sense of dominion does not appear to give one jurisdiction over other men, angels, nor any spiritual beings as is so often portrayed colloquially. Perhaps, what is of the utmost importance is that the concept of dominion is related to honor and respect combined with long life, according to the fifth numerical principle. This is hardly what one would associate with a belligerent occupation.

This type of disparity fosters misunderstandings because words and word usage evolve. Dictionaries and lexicons cover a multitude of texts to formulate the definitions. The Torah, on the other hand, is the vocabulary of the Creator; it was presented in one setting. Therefore, there is no evolution of meaning involved. One must learn how the Creator uses his vocabulary throughout the whole of the Torah.

The Hebrew word *yirdoo* (יִרְדּוּ), which is translated *dominion* is only found one time in the Torah; therefore, the comparative analysis must be related to the three-consonant cluster (רדה). An analysis of the first eighteen occurrences involves a family or company of eight word-concepts. Again, it is often considered that one can be better known by the company one keeps, and the company of these three consonants which are first found in *yirdoo* (יִרְדּוּ) is: dominion, divided,

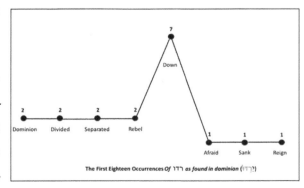

The First Eighteen Occurrences *Of* רדה *as found in dominion* (יִרְדּוּ?)

separated, rebel, down, afraid, sank, and reign. They are tallied as follows: dominion (2), divided (2), separated (2), rebel (2), down (7), afraid (1), sank (1), and reign (1). *Down* dominates the collection, and perhaps, the understanding of dominion is related to an up/down or top/bottom line of thinking.

With that up/down line of thought in mind concerning *down*, the testimony of the pattern of divine perspective can be comparatively embraced. The pattern of divine perspective is a set selection of seven occurrences taken from the first eighteen occurrences of a matter.

The enclosed graphic illustration lists the seven vessels and words, which depict the Creator's perspective concerning these three consonants. Note that the word *down* is the most dominant word-concept in the grouping.

The word-concept *dominion* is (Insert Image_88 right to text) related to a matter of elevation. The Creator is elevated in status above man since the Creator is not a created being. Man is likewise elevated in status above other living creatures because he is created in the image of the Creator. Similarly, as the Creator elevates man by treating him with respect and goodness, man also should elevate the other living creatures of the earth with respect and goodness.

A Summary of The Divine Perspective
on "ירד"
A Pattern of Seven

First: *Foundation*
Ber. 1:26. *And God said. Let us make man in our image, after our likeness, and let them have **dominion** over the fish of the sea, and over the birds of the air, and over the cattle, and over all the earth, and over every creeping thing that creeps upon the earth.* (19 - 3 - 16)

Third: *An Encounter*
Ber. 10:5. *By these were the islands of the nations **divided** in their lands; every one after his tongue, after their families, in their nations.* (9 - 0 - 9)

Seventh: *Completion, Cycle*
Ber. 25:23. *And the Lord said to her, Two nations are in your womb, and two peoples shall be **separated** from your bowels; and the one people shall be stronger than the other people; and the elder shall serve the younger.* (16 - 0 - 16)

Ninth: *A Good Matter, Functioning According To Divine Plan*
Ber. 42:3. *And Joseph's ten brothers **went down** to buy grain in Egypt.* (7 - 1 - 6)

Tenth: *Command, Covenant, or Test*
Ber. 42:28. *And he said to his brothers, My money is restored; and, lo, it is in my sack; and their heart failed them, **and they were afraid**, saying one to another, What is this that God has done to us.* (20 - 3 - 17)

Thirteenth: *Command or Test + A Divine Encounter*
She. 11:8. *And all these your servants **shall come down** to me, and bow down themselves to me, saying, Get out, and all the people who follow you; and after that I will go out. And he went out from Pharaoh in great anger.* (22 - 7 - 15)

Eighteenth: *Command + An Exchange (A life Principle)*
BeM. 16:30. *But if the Lord creates a new thing, and the earth opens her mouth, and swallows them up, with all that belongs to them, **and they go down** alive into Sheol, then you shall understand that these men have provoked the Lord.* (24 - 5 - 19)

The Original Version of the Great Commission

This ninth saying of the ten sayings of creation is the divine perspective on the *authentic version* of the great commission. The generations leading up to the great flood failed to uphold that commission. Likewise, this was the problem at Babel, and probably a significant factor for the dispersion. The nations continually strayed from the great commission, until our father Abraham turned the ebbing tide. His sons, Isaac and Jacob, solidified the absolute nature of the commission. Israel began the journey toward fulfilling the great commission. The Creator designated Israel to be the firstborn nation of the nations. But they fell short of the mark, and they were scattered among the nations. The time will come when Israel shall return and take up the great commission, and function as a *good* firstborn son. They shall then lead the family of nations and the whole of earth's creatures according to the divine design.

Man's Perspective

Man's perspective presently prevails as far as a majority opinion is concerned. The multi-faceted humanistic perspective, whether secular or religious, is focused on the created and not the Creator. Even the monotheistic religions with their multitude of sects are plagued with concepts like heaven, hell, the afterlife, wealth, doctrinal arrogance, and Torah ignorance, their focus is predominantly skewed toward the self and not the Creator. It is mainly all about man, and what is in it for him.

The Nations' Perspective

The nations of the world, for the most part, are driven by man's perspectives, as addressed above. They are focused around their territory, whether it be fear-driven protection or greed induced acquisition. The original divine conception of the great commission is far removed from their strategies.

Israel's Perspective

While many perceive the marvelous resurgence of the secular state of Israel as a fulfillment of some Biblical prophecies, others see it otherwise. From a Biblical perspective, in my opinion, the present secular state of Israel should not be confused with the Biblical nation of Israel. The current Jewish state is not comprised of the whole of Israel. The majority of Israel is still scattered among the nations and shall return in another exodus event of Biblical proportions at the command of the Creator.

Judaism's Perspective

Judaism is not the same as the ancient Israelite religion; it is a sect of Israel that has developed a strategy to maintain a connection to their ancient heritage while living in the diaspora. Although they have marvelously preserved the text of the Torah, they have fabricated their religion upon other writings outside of the Torah text. While they have, for the most part, abandoned idolatry; they are still in the diaspora because of the divine judgment placed upon them.

Before one might consider these comments as fuel for anti-Semitism, one should study and understand the level of holiness that is required to live continuously in the presence of the Creator. Everyone's sins were manifested before the community; if one failed to address those shortcomings adequately, they were found out, and the person or persons were placed outside of the camp, away from the presence, the Creator. Likewise, one should understand that the whole of the nation was held responsible for the actions of every citizen. A prime example of such an incident can be found in Joshua chapter 7 concerning Achan, the thief. The ancient Israelite nation, of which Judaism is forever attached, experienced a level of unprecedented holiness; such a level of holiness shall once again be returned to the nation Israel, and they shall desire to maintain it out of respect for the Creator.

A Maskil's Perspective

A maskil is a man from any nation who seeks to understand and know the Creator according to his Torah (Ps. 14:2).

> *The Lord looked down from heaven upon the children of men, to see if there were any who understand, and seek God:*

A "maskil" is one who is successful in walking according to the ways of the Lord. He also associated with a skilled warrior. Our beloved King David was such a person.

Can One Know the Divine Purpose?

The first collective command given to both male and female humankind was the great commission, the five verbal commands: be fruitful (1), and multiply (2), and replenish (3) the earth, and subdue (4) it; and have dominion (5)...Subduing and having dominion, as demonstrated above, are related to witnessing and elevating the Creator and His commands.

> *And God said, Behold, I have given you every herb bearing seed, which is upon the face of all the earth, and every tree, on which is the fruit of a tree yielding seed; to you it shall be for food: (Bereshiyt 1:29)*

The second collective command follows in the next verse, and it addresses the proper diet for humanity. Of particular notice is the description of kosher and non-kosher regarding fruit. Pardon, the Jewish pun, but kosher refers to what is considered right according to the Torah. Apparently, according to the Hebrew text, a non-kosher fruit would have an exposed seed, perhaps like the modern-day cashew, which is not a nut, but a fruit having an external seed. Possibly, herein lies some insight into the tree of knowledge of good (functional) and evil (dysfunctional). Could it be that the woman did not carefully listen or understand the command concerning the fruit? Maybe, rather than being deceived, she might have been careless concerning the command of the proper food to eat.

Also, the animals were only permitted to eat the green vegetation; they were not allowed to eat of the trees (verse 30). Therefore, it is possible that death entered the animal kingdom first, before the domain of men. Perhaps, the serpent was the first of the animal kingdom to eat non-kosher food. One might ask, where is the death of animals found in the garden discussion?

Bereshiyt 3:21. For Adam and for his wife, the Lord God made coats of skins, and clothed them:

Of course, these are mainly assumptions, but they are founded upon reasonable questions that are raised from the text. What may be taken to be instincts may be related to programmed commands from the Creator. Could it be that even the animals have some portion in the scope of free will?

The bottom line of this reasoning is that the Creator's purpose was given to man and the living creatures. Therefore, His will was meant to be known.

The Divine Purpose from the Core of the Torah.

Creation's past failures have clouded their understanding of the ways of the Creator. It seems that the correction of those failures may have to follow a top-down approach, meaning it must begin in man. Individual men have experienced some successes before the Creator. However, the creation of the nation of Israel was intended to extend these successes both nationally and internationally. Sadly, the nation of Israel was unable to succeed in that matter collectively. In the height of their wilderness epidemic meltdown, the Creator emphasized most assuredly his purpose for the whole of the world. In the 4,127th vessel of the Torah, the Creator said, and Moses wrote:

Bemidbar (Nu. 14:21)

But as truly as I live, all the earth shall be filled with the glory of the Lord:

<u>There undisputedly is the divine perspective on the divine purpose.</u> The next step is understanding what the glory of the Lord means, according to the Torah. As our Father, the Creator said to Abram, "Go for yourself!" That is a subtle invitation to you, the reader.

Chapter Fifteen

A Commencement Event Is an Ending with A New Beginning

Congratulations! A Diploma Is in Order.

Congratulations are indeed in order, for you have persevered an intense presentation of unfamiliar information. You are genuinely due to a diploma in the foundation of the numerical structure of the Torah. As with all graduation events, they not only mark the end of an endeavor, they also mark the commencement of a new adventure. You now have the foundational skills to navigate the world of the Torah from the numerical perspective.

However, in place of a diploma, this foundational course of numerical studies presents its graduates with a roadmap. This commencement event is the beginning of your adventurous journey, and perhaps this roadmap may be more beneficial than a mere diploma. This roadmap may also serve as a travel brochure to inspire you to proceed on with haste, hone your skills, and perhaps most importantly, guide others along the way.

The Journey Begins Here.

The Torah journey from the unique garden to the land of promise commences with the ordinal numeral two. Why did the Creator choose to begin the Torah with a two? Two is the first number that can be divided by another whole number and yield a whole number. Two, according to the numerical structure of the Torah, relates to division, separation, or two aspects of a matter. Therefore, the Torah begins with the concept of division, which is related to the two aspects of the Creator's creating, the heavens, and the earth.

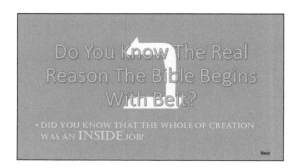

Two is the Hebrew consonant *beit* (ב), which most Hebrew learners associate with a house or dwelling, "*bayit.*" Most English versions of the Torah translate *beit* (ב) with the preposition "in," and they relate "in" to time such as, "In the beginning, God created the heavens and the earth." This standard translation appears to miss the author's intention and usage of both the prepositional ordinal/consonant and the word to which it is prefixed. With both the Creator's purpose and usage in mind, a better translation would be framed in spatial terms rather than with time. Literally, in terms of context, the first word of the Torah, *bereshiyt*, should be translated "inside first of." If this interpretation of the ordinal/consonant *beit* seems to be a bit radical, perhaps Noach could provide some clarity on the issue. If you feel you would like some assistance navigating the varied channels of thought concerning this first word of the Torah, its context, and even Noach's perspective, help is available online.

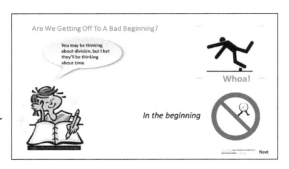

Some Traveling Assistance Is Available.

Assistance is available in video format on YouTube Channel: "Torah123." More specifically, the video "An Investigation Into the Foundation of the Torah" introduces the viewer to the Hebrew word "bereshiyt" in a pleasant and informative manner. There are many

other visually educational videos related to the multiple facets of the numerical structure of the Torah.

Also, the reader is invited to peruse the website www.avipublications. com for many articles related to the numerical structure of the Torah theory and practice. Likewise, the reader is invited to visit www.torah123.com for lessons from the Torah based upon the numerical structure of the Torah.

Videos: YouTube Channel: "Torah123"
Numerical Structure Articles: www.avipublications.com
Torah Articles (numerical perspective): www.torah123.com
Book Blog: www.numericalstructureofthetorah.com

Lastly, of course, is our book blog at the www.numericalstructureofthetorah. com, which is dedicated to the ongoing discussion of the entire content of this book.

Videos: YOUTUBE Channel: Torah123

Numerical Structure Articles: avipublications.com

Torah Articles (numerical perspective): torah123.com

Book Blog: numericalstructureofthetorah.com

Happy Motoring! Don't Forget the Roadmap!

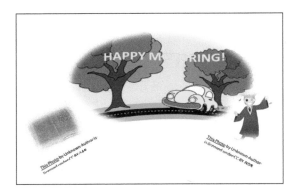

About Avi Publications

For reasons that I cannot explain, I have been blessed from my childhood to know God as my loving Father. I was not raised in any form of religious culture, but somehow, I always knew that I am not alone, and He is there for me.

My life has been full of problems, some of which I could control, and some which were beyond my ability to control. It is those problems which were beyond my control, that I know now, were special blessings in disguise. Those problems caused me to turn my whole being toward my loving Father, and as any good father should, He came to my rescue with love, discipline, and respect. I have and always shall expect to hear the voice of my Father (avi) in response to my requests. He is first my Father; secondly, He is my master (my teacher), and most certainly, He is my God.

We both have high expectations of each other, I am all about the here and now, and so is He. I expect him to be a father to me here and now, and I know that He expects me to be a son to Him, here and now. I am talking about what a son should be, not just a son because I exist. The first son, Cain, did not respect the counsel of his Father, and he was banned from the presence of his Father. He was also deleted from the family genealogy. His family tree consists of the sons of men.

I am only one of a multitude of people in whom the voice of the Creator is making himself known, people who desire his parental instruction. Why all of this is coming about, I can only guess. The religious hurdles that these returning pilgrims encounter are formidable, but their Father is waiting for them with an outstretched arm. It is their Father whom they seek, and no present religious institution can afford them the truths concerning the relationship, which they so desire. From the great religions of the world, they are coming, and their desire is for His teachings (Torah).

Avi **Publications** is dedicated to learning the Torah solely from the text of the Torah, utilizing the numerical structure of the Torah as our guide. *Avi* Publications has high expectations of ourselves as sons and daughters, and of the Creator as our Father. These expectations are a family matter, and as loving, functional family members, we shall become shining reflections of our Father's glory.

Please visit www.avipublications.com and YouTube channel "**Torah123**" for more new articles, and videos related to the numerical structure of the Torah.

Appendix

The Twenty Absolute Vessel Formulations

1. A Sequential Listing of the Vessel Formulation (3-0-3)

Thirteen Vessels

Vessel	Book	Chp.	Vs.	Form.
673	*Bereshiyt*	25	14	3-0-3
699	*Bereshiyt*	26	6	3-0-3
1,292	*Bereshiyt*	43	1	3-0-3
1,492	*Bereshiyt*	49	18	3-0-3
1,536	*Shemot*	1	3	3-0-3
2,129	*Shemot*	22	17	3-0-3
2,304	*Shemot*	28	13	3-0-3
3,164	*VaYikra*	14	55	3-0-3
3,165	*VaYikra*	14	56	3-0-3
3,845	*BeMidbar*	6	24	3-0-3
4,495	*BeMidbar*	26	8	3-0-3
5,611	*Devarim*	28	5	3-0-3
5,623	*Devarim*	28	17	3-0-3

2. *A Sequential Listing of the Vessel Formulation (4-0-4)*

Thirty-Seven Vessels

Vessel	Book	Chp.	Vs.	Form.
538	Bereshiyt	21	24	4-0-4
618	Bereshiyt	24	26	4-0-4
626	Bereshiyt	24	34	4-0-4
716	Bereshiyt	26	23	4-0-4
1,036	Bereshiyt	35	24	4-0-4
1,535	Shemot	1	2	4-0-4
1,537	Shemot	1	4	4-0-4
1,933	Shemot	15	12	4-0-4
1,939	Shemot	15	18	4-0-4
1,978	Shemot	16	30	4-0-4
1,984	Shemot	16	36	4-0-4
2,145	Shemot	23	3	4-0-4
2,231	Shemot	25	38	4-0-4
2,995	VaYikra	10	20	4-0-4
3,356	VaYikra	21	13	4-0-4
4,126	BeMidbar	14	20	4-0-4
4,357	BeMidbar	21	19	4-0-4
4,369	BeMidbar	21	31	4-0-4
4,695	BeMidbar	31	33	4-0-4

Vessel	Book	Chp.	Vs.	Form.
4,696	BeMidbar	31	34	4-0-4
4,706	BeMidbar	31	44	4-0-4
4,771	BeMidbar	33	13	4-0-4
4,776	BeMidbar	33	18	4-0-4
4,779	BeMidbar	33	21	4-0-4
4,780	BeMidbar	33	22	4-0-4
4,783	BeMidbar	33	25	4-0-4
4,784	BeMidbar	33	26	4-0-4
4,785	BeMidbar	33	27	4-0-4
4,786	BeMidbar	33	28	4-0-4
4,787	BeMidbar	33	29	4-0-4
4,788	BeMidbar	33	30	4-0-4
4,792	BeMidbar	33	34	4-0-4
4,800	BeMidbar	33	42	4-0-4
4,801	BeMidbar	33	43	4-0-4
4,938	Devarim	2	2	4-0-4
4,953	Devarim	2	17	4-0-4
5,769	Devarim	32	16	4-0-4

3. *A Sequential Listing of the Vessel Formulation (5-0-5)*

Sixty-Eight Vessels

Vessel	Book	Chp.	Vs.	Form.
146	Bereshiyt	6	8	5-0-5
238	Bereshiyt	10	3	5-0-5
308	Bereshiyt	12	9	5-0-5
367	Bereshiyt	15	6	5-0-5
674	Bereshiyt	25	15	5-0-5
723	Bereshiyt	26	30	5-0-5
728	Bereshiyt	26	35	5-0-5
836	Bereshiyt	30	5	5-0-5
859	Bereshiyt	30	28	5-0-5
919	Bereshiyt	31	45	5-0-5
967	Bereshiyt	33	6	5-0-5
973	Bereshiyt	33	12	5-0-5
1,042	Bereshiyt	36	1	5-0-5
1,398	Bereshiyt	46	11	5-0-5
1,401	Bereshiyt	46	14	5-0-5
1,497	Bereshiyt	49	23	5-0-5
1,673	Shemot	6	17	5-0-5
1,677	Shemot	6	21	5-0-5
1,678	Shemot	6	22	5-0-5
1,760	Shemot	9	17	5-0-5
1,872	Shemot	13	4	5-0-5
1,904	Shemot	14	14	5-0-5
1,924	Shemot	15	3	5-0-5
2,076	Shemot	21	1	5-0-5

Vessel	Book	Chp.	Vs.	Form.
2,087	Shemot	21	12	5-0-5
2,090	Shemot	21	15	5-0-5
2,092	Shemot	21	17	5-0-5
2,148	Shemot	23	6	5-0-5
2,156	Shemot	23	14	5-0-5
2,201	Shemot	25	8	5-0-5
2,309	Shemot	28	18	5-0-5
2,310	Shemot	28	19	5-0-5
2,485	Shemot	33	14	5-0-5
2,502	Shemot	34	8	5-0-5
2,644	Shemot	38	13	5-0-5
2,673	Shemot	39	11	5-0-5
2,674	Shemot	39	12	5-0-5
2,847	VaYikra	5	19	5-0-5
2,947	VaYikra	8	32	5-0-5
3,025	VaYikra	11	30	5-0-5
3,045	VaYikra	12	3	5-0-5
3,224	VaYikra	16	25	5-0-5
3,347	VaYikra	21	4	5-0-5
3,846	BeMidbar	6	25	5-0-5
4,138	BeMidbar	14	32	5-0-5
4,348	BeMidbar	21	10	5-0-5
4,360	BeMidbar	21	12	5-0-5
4,473	BeMidbar	24	19	5-0-5
4,515	BeMidbar	26	28	5-0-5
4,597	BeMidbar	28	22	5-0-5
4,605	BeMidbar	28	30	5-0-5
4,707	BeMidbar	31	45	5-0-5

Vessel	Book	Chp.	Vs.	Form.
4,708	BeMidbar	31	46	5-0-5
4,715	BeMidbar	31	53	5-0-5
4,773	BeMidbar	33	15	5-0-5
4,775	BeMidbar	33	17	5-0-5
4,777	BeMidbar	33	19	5-0-5
4,778	BeMidbar	33	20	5-0-5
4,789	BeMidbar	33	31	5-0-5
4,791	BeMidbar	33	33	5-0-5
4,793	BeMidbar	33	35	5-0-5
4,799	BeMidbar	33	41	5-0-5
4,803	BeMidbar	33	45	5-0-5
5,002	Devarim	3	29	5-0-5
5,303	Devarim	14	18	5-0-5
5,392	Devarim	18	13	5-0-5
5,779	Devarim	32	26	5-0-5
5,830	Devarim	33	25	5-0-5

4. *A Sequential Listing of the Vessel Formulation (6-0-6)*

One Hundred Twenty-Four Vessels

Vessel	Book	Chp.	Vs.	Form.
226	Bereshiyt	9	20	6-0-6
239	Bereshiyt	10	4	6-0-6
241	Bereshiyt	10	6	6-0-6
258	Bereshiyt	10	23	6-0-6
297	Bereshiyt	11	30	6-0-6
321	Bereshiyt	13	2	6-0-6

Vessel	Book	Chp.	Vs.	Form.
332	Bereshiyt	13	13	6-0-6
484	Bereshiyt	19	26	6-0-6
548	Bereshiyt	21	34	6-0-6
660	Bereshiyt	25	1	6-0-6
683	Bereshiyt	25	24	6-0-6
763	Bereshiyt	27	35	6-0-6
784	Bereshiyt	28	10	6-0-6
841	Bereshiyt	30	10	6-0-6
865	Bereshiyt	30	34	6-0-6
977	Bereshiyt	33	16	6-0-6
1,037	Bereshiyt	35	25	6-0-6
1,077	Bereshiyt	36	36	6-0-6
1,082	Bereshiyt	36	41	6-0-6
1,083	Bereshiyt	36	42	6-0-6
1,147	Bereshiyt	38	27	6-0-6
1,243	Bereshiyt	41	47	6-0-6
1,328	Bereshiyt	44	3	6-0-6
1,396	Bereshiyt	46	9	6-0-6
1,400	Bereshiyt	46	13	6-0-6
1,406	Bereshiyt	46	19	6-0-6
1,411	Bereshiyt	46	24	6-0-6
1,479	Bereshiyt	49	5	6-0-6
1,488	Bereshiyt	49	14	6-0-6
1,490	Bereshiyt	49	16	6-0-6
1,493	Bereshiyt	49	19	6-0-6
1,519	Bereshiyt	50	12	6-0-6
1,725	Shemot	8	10	6-0-6
1,888	Shemot	13	20	6-0-6
2,058	Shemot	20	6	6-0-6

Vessel	Book	Chp.	Vs.	Form.
2,131	Shemot	22	19	6-0-6
2,197	Shemot	25	4	6-0-6
2,227	Shemot	25	34	6-0-6
2,255	Shemot	26	22	6-0-6
2,256	Shemot	26	23	6-0-6
2,377	Shemot	29	43	6-0-6
2,422	Shemot	31	4	6-0-6
2,535	Shemot	35	6	6-0-6
2,561	Shemot	35	32	6-0-6
2,591	Shemot	36	27	6-0-6
2,592	Shemot	36	28	6-0-6
2,622	Shemot	37	20	6-0-6
2,787	VaYikra	3	11	6-0-6
2,878	VaYikra	7	1	6-0-6
3,064	VaYikra	13	14	6-0-6
3,386	VaYikra	22	19	6-0-6
3,398	VaYikra	22	31	6-0-6
3,465	VaYikra	24	21	6-0-6
3,491	VaYikra	25	24	6-0-6
3,551	VaYikra	26	29	6-0-6
3,560	VaYikra	26	38	6-0-6
3,649	BeMidbar	1	47	6-0-6
3,675	BeMidbar	2	19	6-0-6
3,677	BeMidbar	2	21	6-0-6
3,713	BeMidbar	3	23	6-0-6
3,727	BeMidbar	3	37	6-0-6
3,765	BeMidbar	4	24	6-0-6
3,779	BeMidbar	4	38	6-0-6
3,785	BeMidbar	4	44	6-0-6

Vessel	Book	Chp.	Vs.	Form.
3,806	BeMidbar	5	16	6-0-6
3,829	BeMidbar	6	8	6-0-6
3,862	BeMidbar	7	14	6-0-6
3,868	BeMidbar	7	20	6-0-6
3,874	BeMidbar	7	26	6-0-6
3,880	BeMidbar	7	32	6-0-6
3,886	BeMidbar	7	38	6-0-6
3,892	BeMidbar	7	44	6-0-6
3,898	BeMidbar	7	50	6-0-6
3,904	BeMidbar	7	56	6-0-6
3,910	BeMidbar	7	62	6-0-6
3,916	BeMidbar	7	68	6-0-6
3,922	BeMidbar	7	74	6-0-6
3,928	BeMidbar	7	80	6-0-6
3,991	BeMidbar	10	5	6-0-6
4,098	BeMidbar	13	25	6-0-6
4,172	BeMidbar	15	21	6-0-6
4,434	BeMidbar	23	20	6-0-6
4,436	BeMidbar	23	22	6-0-6
4,478	BeMidbar	25	9	6-0-6
4,493	BeMidbar	26	6	6-0-6
4,500	BeMidbar	26	13	6-0-6
4,503	BeMidbar	26	16	6-0-6
4,504	BeMidbar	26	17	6-0-6
4,511	BeMidbar	26	24	6-0-6
4,518	BeMidbar	26	31	6-0-6
4,519	BeMidbar	26	32	6-0-6
4,523	BeMidbar	26	36	6-0-6
4,526	BeMidbar	26	39	6-0-6

Vessel	Book	Chp.	Vs.	Form.
4,536	BeMidbar	26	49	6-0-6
4,540	BeMidbar	26	53	6-0-6
4,604	BeMidbar	28	29	6-0-6
4,610	BeMidbar	29	4	6-0-6
4,616	BeMidbar	29	10	6-0-6
4,774	BeMidbar	33	16	6-0-6
4,790	BeMidbar	33	32	6-0-6
4,804	BeMidbar	33	46	6-0-6
4,902	Devarim	1	12	6-0-6
4,922	Devarim	1	32	6-0-6
5,053	Devarim	5	2	6-0-6
5,061	Devarim	5	10	6-0-6
5,078	Devarim	5	27	6-0-6
5,085	Devarim	6	4	6-0-6
5,218	Devarim	11	15	6-0-6
5,396	Devarim	18	17	6-0-6
5,476	Devarim	22	11	6-0-6
5,552	Devarim	25	10	6-0-6
5,609	Devarim	28	3	6-0-6
5,612	Devarim	28	6	6-0-6
5,622	Devarim	28	16	6-0-6
5,625	Devarim	28	19	6-0-6
5,634	Devarim	28	28	6-0-6
5,640	Devarim	28	34	6-0-6
5,771	Devarim	32	18	6-0-6
5,772	Devarim	32	19	6-0-6
5,782	Devarim	32	29	6-0-6
5,784	Devarim	32	31	6-0-6
5,786	Devarim	32	33	6-0-6

Vessel	Book	Chp.	Vs.	Form.
5,790	Devarim	32	37	6-0-6
5,819	Devarim	33	14	6-0-6

5. *A Sequential Listing of the Vessel Formulation (7-0-7)*

Ninety-Eight Vessels

Vessel	Book	Chp.	Vs.	Form.
1	Bereshiyt	1	1	7-0-7
56	Bereshiyt	2	25	7-0-7
149	Bereshiyt	6	11	7-0-7
231	Bereshiyt	9	25	7-0-7
257	Bereshiyt	10	22	7-0-7
265	Bereshiyt	10	30	7-0-7
369	Bereshiyt	15	8	7-0-7
420	Bereshiyt	17	22	7-0-7
424	Bereshiyt	17	26	7-0-7
464	Bereshiyt	19	6	7-0-7
620	Bereshiyt	24	28	7-0-7
752	Bereshiyt	27	24	7-0-7
843	Bereshiyt	30	12	7-0-7
896	Bereshiyt	31	22	7-0-7
1,040	Bereshiyt	35	28	7-0-7
1,049	Bereshiyt	36	8	7-0-7
1,050	Bereshiyt	36	9	7-0-7
1,067	Bereshiyt	36	26	7-0-7
1,075	Bereshiyt	36	34	7-0-7
1,078	Bereshiyt	36	37	7-0-7

Vessel	Book	Chp.	Vs.	Form.
1,085	Bereshiyt	37	1	7-0-7
1,126	Bereshiyt	38	6	7-0-7
1,135	Bereshiyt	38	15	7-0-7
1,284	Bereshiyt	42	31	7-0-7
1,322	Bereshiyt	43	31	7-0-7
1,553	Shemot	1	20	7-0-7
1,604	Shemot	4	2	7-0-7
1,626	Shemot	4	24	7-0-7
1,628	Shemot	4	26	7-0-7
1,775	Shemot	9	32	7-0-7
1,866	Shemot	12	49	7-0-7
1,935	Shemot	15	14	7-0-7
1,999	Shemot	17	15	7-0-7
2,091	Shemot	21	16	7-0-7
2,139	Shemot	22	27	7-0-7
2,198	Shemot	25	5	7-0-7
2,199	Shemot	25	6	7-0-7
2,206	Shemot	25	13	7-0-7
2,208	Shemot	25	15	7-0-7
2,253	Shemot	26	20	7-0-7
2,283	Shemot	27	13	7-0-7
2,307	Shemot	28	16	7-0-7
2,379	Shemot	29	45	7-0-7
2,536	Shemot	35	7	7-0-7
2,537	Shemot	35	8	7-0-7
2,606	Shemot	37	4	7-0-7
2,888	VaYikra	7	11	7-0-7
2,894	VaYikra	7	17	7-0-7
3,284	VaYikra	19	5	7-0-7

Vessel	Book	Chp.	Vs.	Form.
3,323	VaYikra	20	7	7-0-7
3,532	VaYikra	26	10	7-0-7
3,635	BeMidbar	1	33	7-0-7
3,637	BeMidbar	1	35	7-0-7
3,660	BeMidbar	2	4	7-0-7
3,662	BeMidbar	2	6	7-0-7
3,664	BeMidbar	2	8	7-0-7
3,667	BeMidbar	2	11	7-0-7
3,669	BeMidbar	2	13	7-0-7
3,679	BeMidbar	2	23	7-0-7
3,682	BeMidbar	2	26	7-0-7
3,684	BeMidbar	2	28	7-0-7
3,686	BeMidbar	2	30	7-0-7
3,709	BeMidbar	3	19	7-0-7
3,738	BeMidbar	3	48	7-0-7
3,777	BeMidbar	4	36	7-0-7
3,783	BeMidbar	4	42	7-0-7
3,789	BeMidbar	4	48	7-0-7
3,847	BeMidbar	6	26	7-0-7
4,022	BeMidbar	10	36	7-0-7
4,057	BeMidbar	11	35	7-0-7
4,073	BeMidbar	12	16	1-0-1
4,163	BeMidbar	15	12	7-0-7
4,170	BeMidbar	15	19	7-0-7
4,213	BeMidbar	16	21	7-0-7
4,501	BeMidbar	26	14	7-0-7
4,596	BeMidbar	28	21	7-0-7
4,621	BeMidbar	29	15	7-0-7
4,624	BeMidbar	29	18	7-0-7

Vessel	Book	Chp.	Vs.	Form.
4,627	BeMidbar	29	21	7-0-7
4,630	BeMidbar	29	24	7-0-7
4,633	BeMidbar	29	27	7-0-7
4,636	BeMidbar	29	30	7-0-7
4,639	BeMidbar	29	33	7-0-7
4,643	BeMidbar	29	37	7-0-7
4,691	BeMidbar	31	29	7-0-7
4,764	BeMidbar	33	6	7-0-7
4,802	BeMidbar	33	44	7-0-7
4,814	BeMidbar	33	56	7-0-7
4,824	BeMidbar	34	10	7-0-7
4,936	Devarim	1	46	7-0-7
5,006	Devarim	4	4	7-0-7
5,229	Devarim	11	26	7-0-7
5,290	Devarim	14	5	7-0-7
5,336	Devarim	15	22	7-0-7
5,756	Devarim	32	3	7-0-7
5,762	Devarim	32	9	7-0-7
5,765	Devarim	32	12	7-0-7
5,823	Devarim	33	18	7-0-7

6. *A Sequential Listing of the Vessel Formulation (8-0-8)*

Eighty-Eight Vessels

Vessel	Book	Chp.	Vs.	Form.
43	Bereshiyt	2	12	8-0-8
77	Bereshiyt	3	21	8-0-8

Vessel	Book	Chp.	Vs.	Form.
180	Bereshiyt	7	20	8-0-8
198	Bereshiyt	8	14	8-0-8
301	Bereshiyt	12	2	8-0-8
336	Bereshiyt	13	17	8-0-8
400	Bereshiyt	17	2	8-0-8
402	Bereshiyt	17	4	8-0-8
434	Bereshiyt	18	9	8-0-8
442	Bereshiyt	18	17	8-0-8
511	Bereshiyt	20	15	8-0-8
525	Bereshiyt	21	11	8-0-8
736	Bereshiyt	27	8	8-0-8
738	Bereshiyt	27	10	8-0-8
885	Bereshiyt	31	11	8-0-8
902	Bereshiyt	31	28	8-0-8
943	Bereshiyt	32	15	8-0-8
1,031	Bereshiyt	35	19	8-0-8
1,052	Bereshiyt	36	11	8-0-8
1,064	Bereshiyt	36	23	8-0-8
1,105	Bereshiyt	37	21	8-0-8
1,139	Bereshiyt	38	19	8-0-8
1,179	Bereshiyt	40	6	8-0-8
1,195	Bereshiyt	40	22	8-0-8
1,202	Bereshiyt	41	6	8-0-8
1,249	Bereshiyt	41	53	8-0-8
1,319	Bereshiyt	43	28	8-0-8
1,423	Bereshiyt	47	2	8-0-8
1,464	Bereshiyt	48	12	8-0-8
1,675	Shemot	6	19	8-0-8
1,680	Shemot	6	24	8-0-8

Vessel	Book	Chp.	Vs.	Form.
1,774	Shemot	9	31	8-0-8
1,874	Shemot	13	6	8-0-8
1,927	Shemot	15	6	8-0-8
1,928	Shemot	15	7	8-0-8
1,931	Shemot	15	10	8-0-8
2,024	Shemot	18	24	8-0-8
2,184	Shemot	24	9	8-0-8
2,196	Shemot	25	3	8-0-8
2,381	Shemot	30	1	8-0-8
2,404	Shemot	30	24	8-0-8
2,589	Shemot	36	25	8-0-8
2,766	VaYikra	2	6	8-0-8
2,775	VaYikra	2	15	8-0-8
2,882	VaYikra	7	5	8-0-8
2,909	VaYikra	7	32	8-0-8
3,089	VaYikra	13	40	8-0-8
3,166	VaYikra	14	57	8-0-8
3,249	VaYikra	17	16	8-0-8
3,486	VaYikra	25	19	8-0-8
3,623	BeMidbar	1	21	8-0-8
3,625	BeMidbar	1	23	8-0-8
3,629	BeMidbar	1	27	8-0-8
3,631	BeMidbar	1	29	8-0-8
3,633	BeMidbar	1	31	8-0-8
3,639	BeMidbar	1	37	8-0-8
3,641	BeMidbar	1	39	8-0-8
3,643	BeMidbar	1	41	8-0-8
3,645	BeMidbar	1	43	8-0-8
3,671	BeMidbar	2	15	8-0-8

Vessel	Book	Chp.	Vs.	Form.
4,253	BeMidbar	17	26	8-0-8
4,388	BeMidbar	22	15	8-0-8
4,467	BeMidbar	24	23	8-0-8
4,471	BeMidbar	25	2	8-0-8
4,514	BeMidbar	26	27	8-0-8
4,532	BeMidbar	26	45	8-0-8
4,591	BeMidbar	28	16	8-0-8
4,628	BeMidbar	29	22	8-0-8
4,634	BeMidbar	29	28	8-0-8
4,637	BeMidbar	29	31	8-0-8
4,640	BeMidbar	29	34	8-0-8
4,644	BeMidbar	29	38	8-0-8
4,700	BeMidbar	31	38	8-0-8
4,795	BeMidbar	33	37	8-0-8
4,805	BeMidbar	33	47	8-0-8
4,819	BeMidbar	34	5	8-0-8
4,872	BeMidbar	35	29	8-0-8
4,971	Devarim	2	35	8-0-8
4,995	Devarim	3	22	8-0-8
5,026	Devarim	4	24	8-0-8
5,055	Devarim	5	4	8-0-8
5,197	Devarim	10	16	8-0-8
5,304	Devarim	14	19	8-0-8
5,507	Devarim	23	13	8-0-8
5,567	Devarim	26	6	8-0-8
5,587	Devarim	27	7	8-0-8
5,758	Devarim	32	5	8-0-8
5,831	Devarim	33	26	8-0-8

One Hundred Twenty-One Vessels

Vessel	Book	Chp.	Vs.	Form.
83	Bereshiyt	4	3	9-0-9
160	Bereshiyt	6	22	9-0-9
232	Bereshiyt	9	26	9-0-9
237	Bereshiyt	10	2	9-0-9
240	Bereshiyt	10	5	9-0-9
245	Bereshiyt	10	10	9-0-9
269	Bereshiyt	11	2	9-0-9
302	Bereshiyt	12	3	9-0-9
356	Bereshiyt	14	19	9-0-9
404	Bereshiyt	17	6	9-0-9
409	Bereshiyt	17	11	9-0-9
541	Bereshiyt	21	27	9-0-9
566	Bereshiyt	22	18	9-0-9
684	Bereshiyt	25	25	9-0-9
777	Bereshiyt	28	3	9-0-9
782	Bereshiyt	28	8	9-0-9
800	Bereshiyt	29	4	9-0-9
812	Bereshiyt	29	16	9-0-9
838	Bereshiyt	30	7	9-0-9
873	Bereshiyt	30	42	9-0-9
914	Bereshiyt	31	40	9-0-9
953	Bereshiyt	32	25	9-0-9
991	Bereshiyt	34	10	9-0-9
1,089	Bereshiyt	37	5	9-0-9

Vessel	Book	Chp.	Vs.	Form.
1,102	Bereshiyt	37	18	9-0-9
1,108	Bereshiyt	37	24	9-0-9
1,127	Bereshiyt	38	7	9-0-9
1,133	Bereshiyt	38	13	9-0-9
1,168	Bereshiyt	39	18	9-0-9
1,216	Bereshiyt	41	20	9-0-9
1,219	Bereshiyt	41	23	9-0-9
1,276	Bereshiyt	42	23	9-0-9
1,337	Bereshiyt	44	12	9-0-9
1,403	Bereshiyt	46	16	9-0-9
1,501	Bereshiyt	49	27	9-0-9
1,692	Shemot	7	6	9-0-9
1,699	Shemot	7	13	9-0-9
1,722	Shemot	8	7	9-0-9
1,773	Shemot	9	30	9-0-9
2,054	Shemot	20	2	9-0-9
2,100	Shemot	21	25	9-0-9
2,217	Shemot	25	24	9-0-9
2,229	Shemot	25	36	9-0-9
2,276	Shemot	27	6	9-0-9
2,280	Shemot	27	10	9-0-9
2,284	Shemot	27	14	9-0-9
2,285	Shemot	27	15	9-0-9
2,311	Shemot	28	20	9-0-9
2,415	Shemot	30	35	9-0-9
2,499	Shemot	34	5	9-0-9
2,515	Shemot	34	21	9-0-9
2,613	Shemot	37	11	9-0-9

Vessel	Book	Chp.	Vs.	Form.
2,624	Shemot	37	22	9-0-9
2,636	Shemot	38	5	9-0-9
2,641	Shemot	38	10	9-0-9
2,675	Shemot	39	13	9-0-9
2,721	Shemot	40	16	9-0-9
2,722	Shemot	40	17	9-0-9
2,741	Shemot	40	36	9-0-9
2,747	VaYikra	1	4	9-0-9
2,914	VaYikra	7	37	9-0-9
2,927	VaYikra	8	12	9-0-9
2,949	VaYikra	8	34	9-0-9
2,952	VaYikra	9	1	9-0-9
2,977	VaYikra	10	2	9-0-9
2,985	VaYikra	10	10	9-0-9
3,003	VaYikra	11	8	9-0-9
3,091	VaYikra	13	41	9-0-9
3,286	VaYikra	19	7	9-0-9
3,306	VaYikra	19	27	9-0-9
3,400	VaYikra	22	33	9-0-9
3,405	VaYikra	23	5	9-0-9
3,499	VaYikra	25	32	9-0-9
3,619	BeMidbar	1	17	9-0-9
3,627	BeMidbar	1	25	9-0-9
3,711	BeMidbar	3	21	9-0-9
3,723	BeMidbar	3	33	9-0-9
3,781	BeMidbar	4	40	9-0-9
3,819	BeMidbar	5	29	9-0-9
3,962	BeMidbar	8	25	9-0-9

Vessel	Book	Chp.	Vs.	Form.
4,049	BeMidbar	11	27	9-0-9
4,167	BeMidbar	15	16	9-0-9
4,246	BeMidbar	17	19	9-0-9
4,353	BeMidbar	21	15	9-0-9
4,374	BeMidbar	22	1	9-0-9
4,397	BeMidbar	22	24	9-0-9
4,413	BeMidbar	22	40	9-0-9
4,444	BeMidbar	23	30	9-0-9
4,506	BeMidbar	26	19	9-0-9
4,509	BeMidbar	26	22	9-0-9
4,510	BeMidbar	26	23	9-0-9
4,512	BeMidbar	26	25	9-0-9
4,517	BeMidbar	26	30	9-0-9
4,521	BeMidbar	26	34	9-0-9
4,535	BeMidbar	26	48	9-0-9
4,580	BeMidbar	28	5	9-0-9
4,581	BeMidbar	28	6	9-0-9
4,666	BeMidbar	31	4	9-0-9
4,701	BeMidbar	31	39	9-0-9
4,719	BeMidbar	32	3	9-0-9
4,806	BeMidbar	33	48	9-0-9
4,822	BeMidbar	34	8	9-0-9
4,900	Devarim	1	10	9-0-9
4,903	Devarim	1	13	9-0-9
4,946	Devarim	2	10	9-0-9
4,963	Devarim	2	27	9-0-9
5,043	Devarim	4	41	9-0-9
5,057	Devarim	5	6	9-0-9

Vessel	Book	Chp.	Vs.	Form.
5,095	Devarim	6	14	9-0-9
5,129	Devarim	7	23	9-0-9
5,169	Devarim	9	17	9-0-9
5,181	Devarim	9	29	9-0-9
5,289	Devarim	14	4	9-0-9
5,350	Devarim	16	13	9-0-9
5,420	Devarim	19	19	9-0-9
5,492	Devarim	22	27	9-0-9
5,537	Devarim	24	17	9-0-9
5,565	Devarim	26	4	9-0-9
5,644	Devarim	28	38	9-0-9
5,677	Devarim	29	2	9-0-9
5,810	Devarim	33	5	9-0-9

8. *A Sequential Listing of the Vessel Formulation (10-0-10)*

Eighty-Two Vessels

Vessel	Book	Chp.	Vs.	Form.
436	Bereshiyt	18	11	10-0-10
439	Bereshiyt	18	14	10-0-10
447	Bereshiyt	18	22	10-0-10
654	Bereshiyt	24	62	10-0-10
724	Bereshiyt	26	31	10-0-10
742	Bereshiyt	27	14	10-0-10
918	Bereshiyt	31	44	10-0-10
1,035	Bereshiyt	35	23	10-0-10
1,062	Bereshiyt	36	21	10-0-10

Vessel	Book	Chp.	Vs.	Form.
1,117	Bereshiyt	37	33	10-0-10
1,183	Bereshiyt	40	10	10-0-10
1,185	Bereshiyt	40	12	10-0-10
1,191	Bereshiyt	40	18	10-0-10
1,207	Bereshiyt	41	11	10-0-10
1,218	Bereshiyt	41	22	10-0-10
1,267	Bereshiyt	42	14	10-0-10
1,297	Bereshiyt	43	6	10-0-10
1,389	Bereshiyt	46	2	10-0-10
1,477	Bereshiyt	49	3	10-0-10
1,605	Shemot	4	3	10-0-10
1,734	Shemot	8	19	10-0-10
1,748	Shemot	9	5	10-0-10
1,794	Shemot	10	16	10-0-10
1,819	Shemot	12	2	10-0-10
1,893	Shemot	14	3	10-0-10
1,969	Shemot	16	21	10-0-10
2,072	Shemot	20	20	10-0-10
2,135	Shemot	22	23	10-0-10
2,146	Shemot	23	4	10-0-10
2,150	Shemot	23	8	10-0-10
2,192	Shemot	24	17	10-0-10
2,210	Shemot	25	17	10-0-10
2,211	Shemot	25	18	10-0-10
2,247	Shemot	26	14	10-0-10
2,249	Shemot	26	16	10-0-10
2,278	Shemot	27	8	10-0-10
2,327	Shemot	28	36	10-0-10

Vessel	Book	Chp.	Vs.	Form.
2,330	Shemot	28	39	10-0-10
2,382	Shemot	30	2	10-0-10
2,556	Shemot	35	27	10-0-10
2,583	Shemot	36	19	10-0-10
2,585	Shemot	36	21	10-0-10
2,604	Shemot	37	2	10-0-10
2,608	Shemot	37	6	10-0-10
2,609	Shemot	37	7	10-0-10
2,803	VaYikra	4	10	10-0-10
2,873	VaYikra	6	19	10-0-10
3,058	VaYikra	13	8	10-0-10
3,148	VaYikra	14	39	10-0-10
3,264	VaYikra	18	15	10-0-10
3,311	VaYikra	19	32	10-0-10
3,390	VaYikra	22	23	10-0-10
3,391	VaYikra	22	24	10-0-10
3,526	VaYikra	26	4	10-0-10
3,618	BeMidbar	1	16	10-0-10
3,739	BeMidbar	3	49	10-0-10
3,992	BeMidbar	10	6	10-0-10
3,994	BeMidbar	10	8	10-0-10
4,171	BeMidbar	15	20	10-0-10
4,204	BeMidbar	16	12	10-0-10
4,329	BeMidbar	20	20	10-0-10
4,356	BeMidbar	21	18	10-0-10
4,422	BeMidbar	23	8	10-0-10
4,432	BeMidbar	23	18	10-0-10
4,453	BeMidbar	24	9	10-0-10

Vessel	Book	Chp.	Vs.	Form.
4,462	BeMidbar	24	18	10-0-10
4,537	BeMidbar	26	50	10-0-10
4,582	BeMidbar	28	7	10-0-10
4,592	BeMidbar	28	17	10-0-10
4,609	BeMidbar	29	3	10-0-10
4,702	BeMidbar	31	40	10-0-10
4,732	BeMidbar	32	16	10-0-10
4,846	BeMidbar	35	3	10-0-10
4,867	BeMidbar	35	24	10-0-10
5,037	Devarim	4	35	10-0-10
5,088	Devarim	6	7	10-0-10
5,123	Devarim	7	17	10-0-10
5,136	Devarim	8	4	10-0-10
5,199	Devarim	10	18	10-0-10
5,394	Devarim	18	15	10-0-10
5,540	Devarim	24	20	10-0-10
5,541	Devarim	24	21	10-0-10

9. *A Sequential Listing of the Vessel Formulation (11-0-11)*

Eight-Eight Vessels

Vessel	Book	Chp.	Vs.	Form.
6	Bereshiyt	1	6	11-0-11
35	Bereshiyt	2	4	11-0-11
242	Bereshiyt	10	7	11-0-11
274	Bereshiyt	11	7	11-0-11
383	Bereshiyt	16	1	11-0-11

Vessel	Book	Chp.	Vs.	Form.
411	Bereshiyt	17	13	11-0-11
440	Bereshiyt	18	15	11-0-11
647	Bereshiyt	24	55	11-0-11
705	Bereshiyt	26	12	11-0-11
720	Bereshiyt	26	27	11-0-11
740	Bereshiyt	27	12	11-0-11
810	Bereshiyt	29	14	11-0-11
816	Bereshiyt	29	20	11-0-11
888	Bereshiyt	31	14	11-0-11
923	Bereshiyt	31	49	11-0-11
1,070	Bereshiyt	36	29	11-0-11
1,162	Bereshiyt	39	12	11-0-11
1,175	Bereshiyt	40	2	11-0-11
1,201	Bereshiyt	41	5	11-0-11
1,318	Bereshiyt	43	27	11-0-11
1,339	Bereshiyt	44	14	11-0-11
1,366	Bereshiyt	45	7	11-0-11
1,448	Bereshiyt	47	27	11-0-11
1,481	Bereshiyt	49	7	11-0-11
1,482	Bereshiyt	49	8	11-0-11
1,529	Bereshiyt	50	22	11-0-11
1,534	Shemot	1	1	11-0-11
1,540	Shemot	1	7	11-0-11
1,545	Shemot	1	12	11-0-11
1,738	Shemot	8	23	11-0-11
1,811	Shemot	11	4	11-0-11
1,857	Shemot	12	40	11-0-11
1,919	Shemot	14	29	11-0-11

Vessel	Book	Chp.	Vs.	Form.
2,046	Shemot	19	19	11-0-11
2,077	Shemot	21	2	11-0-11
2,216	Shemot	25	23	11-0-11
2,245	Shemot	26	12	11-0-11
2,272	Shemot	27	2	11-0-11
2,275	Shemot	27	5	11-0-11
2,417	Shemot	30	37	11-0-11
2,441	Shemot	32	5	11-0-11
2,516	Shemot	34	22	11-0-11
2,633	Shemot	38	2	11-0-11
2,650	Shemot	38	19	11-0-11
2,998	VaYikra	11	3	11-0-11
3,256	VaYikra	18	7	11-0-11
3,416	VaYikra	23	16	11-0-11
3,450	VaYikra	24	6	11-0-11
3,466	VaYikra	24	22	11-0-11
3,561	VaYikra	26	39	11-0-11
3,580	VaYikra	27	12	11-0-11
3,589	VaYikra	27	21	11-0-11
3,710	BeMidbar	3	20	11-0-11
3,737	BeMidbar	3	47	11-0-11
3,855	BeMidbar	7	7	11-0-11
4,155	BeMidbar	15	4	11-0-11
4,157	BeMidbar	15	6	11-0-11
4,227	BeMidbar	16	35	11-0-11
4,324	BeMidbar	20	15	11-0-11
4,416	BeMidbar	23	2	11-0-11
4,426	BeMidbar	23	12	11-0-11

Vessel	Book	Chp.	Vs.	Form.
4,447	BeMidbar	24	3	11-0-11
4,459	BeMidbar	24	15	11-0-11
4,492	BeMidbar	26	5	11-0-11
4,494	BeMidbar	26	7	11-0-11
4,541	BeMidbar	26	54	11-0-11
4,595	BeMidbar	28	20	11-0-11
4,615	BeMidbar	29	9	11-0-11
4,645	BeMidbar	29	39	11-0-11
4,829	BeMidbar	34	15	11-0-11
4,847	BeMidbar	35	4	11-0-11
4,888	BeMidbar	36	11	11-0-11
4,913	Devarim	1	23	11-0-11
4,957	Devarim	2	21	11-0-11
5,080	Devarim	5	29	11-0-11
5,102	Devarim	6	21	11-0-11
5,488	Devarim	22	23	11-0-11
5,569	Devarim	26	8	11-0-11
5,649	Devarim	28	43	11-0-11
5,650	Devarim	28	44	11-0-11
5,672	Devarim	28	66	11-0-11
5,685	Devarim	29	10	11-0-11
5,686	Devarim	29	11	11-0-11
5,763	Devarim	32	10	11-0-11
5,818	Devarim	33	13	11-0-11
5,828	Devarim	33	23	11-0-11
5,829	Devarim	33	24	11-0-11
5,832	Devarim	33	27	11-0-11

10. A Sequential Listing of the Vessel Formulation (12-0-12)

Seventy-Eight Vessels

Vessel	Book	Chp.	Vs.	Form.
45	Bereshiyt	2	14	12-0-12
107	Bereshiyt	5	1	12-0-12
187	Bereshiyt	8	3	12-0-12
305	Bereshiyt	12	6	12-0-12
370	Bereshiyt	15	9	12-0-12
573	Bereshiyt	23	1	12-0-12
623	Bereshiyt	24	31	12-0-12
655	Bereshiyt	24	63	12-0-12
672	Bereshiyt	25	13	12-0-12
790	Bereshiyt	28	16	12-0-12
815	Bereshiyt	29	19	12-0-12
925	Bereshiyt	31	51	12-0-12
929	Bereshiyt	32	1	12-0-12
944	Bereshiyt	32	16	12-0-12
1,071	Bereshiyt	36	30	12-012
1,203	Bereshiyt	41	7	12-0-12
1,332	Bereshiyt	44	7	12-0-12
1,404	Bereshiyt	46	17	12-0-12
1,408	Bereshiyt	46	21	12-0-12
1,483	Bereshiyt	49	9	12-0-12
1,548	Shemot	1	15	12-0-12
1,644	Shemot	5	11	12-0-12
1,686	Shemot	6	30	12-0-12
1,742	Shemot	8	27	12-0-12

Vessel	Book	Chp.	Vs.	Form.
1,876	Shemot	13	8	12-0-12
1,930	Shemot	15	9	12-0-12
1,936	Shemot	15	15	12-0-12
1,938	Shemot	15	17	12-0-12
1,995	Shemot	17	11	12-0-12
2,088	Shemot	21	13	12-0-12
2,099	Shemot	21	24	12-0-12
2,185	Shemot	24	10	12-0-12
2,204	Shemot	25	11	12-0-12
2,222	Shemot	25	29	12-0-12
2,269	Shemot	26	36	12-0-12
2,331	Shemot	28	40	12-0-12
2,442	Shemot	32	6	12-0-12
2,508	Shemot	34	14	12-0-12
2,601	Shemot	36	37	12-0-12
2,864	VaYikra	6	10	12-0-12
2,912	VaYikra	7	35	12-0-12
3,061	VaYikra	13	11	12-0-12
3,120	VaYikra	14	11	12-0-12
3,307	VaYikra	19	28	12-0-12
3,406	VaYikra	23	6	12-0-12
3,449	VaYikra	24	5	12-0-12
3,473	VaYikra	25	6	12-0-12
3,530	VaYikra	26	8	12-0-12
3,555	VaYikra	26	33	12-0-12
3,836	BeMidbar	6	15	12-0-12
3,997	BeMidbar	10	11	12-0-12
4,021	BeMidbar	10	35	12-0-12

Vessel	Book	Chp.	Vs.	Form.
4,062	BeMidbar	12	5	12-0-12
4,180	BeMidbar	15	29	12-0-12
4,231	BeMidbar	17	4	12-0-12
4,499	BeMidbar	26	12	12-0-12
4,502	BeMidbar	26	15	12-0-12
4,513	BeMidbar	26	26	12-0-12
4,525	BeMidbar	26	38	12-0-12
4,531	BeMidbar	26	44	12-0-12
4,603	BeMidbar	28	28	12-0-12
4,676	BeMidbar	31	14	12-0-12
4,720	BeMidbar	32	4	12-0-12
4,748	BeMidbar	32	32	12-0-12
5,203	Devarim	10	22	12-0-12
5,281	Devarim	13	15	12-0-12
5,344	Devarim	16	7	12-0-12
5,345	Devarim	16	8	12-0-12
5,403	Devarim	19	2	12-0-12
5,413	Devarim	19	12	12-0-12
5,518	Devarim	23	24	12-0-12
5,628	Devarim	28	22	12-0-12
5,733	Devarim	31	10	12-0-12
5,761	Devarim	32	8	12-0-12
5,768	Devarim	32	15	12-0-12
5,791	Devarim	32	38	12-0-12
5,795	Devarim	32	42	12-0-12
5,821	Devarim	33	16	12-0-12

11. A Sequential Listing of the Vessel Formulation (13-0-13)

Sixty-Four Vessels

Vessel	Book	Chp.	Vs.	Form.
48	Bereshiyt	2	17	13-0-13
63	Bereshiyt	3	7	13-0-13
189	Bereshiyt	8	5	13-0-13
318	Bereshiyt	12	19	13-0-13
510	Bereshiyt	20	14	13-0-13
574	Bereshiyt	23	2	13-0-13
608	Bereshiyt	24	16	13-0-13
767	Bereshiyt	27	39	13-0-13
912	Bereshiyt	31	38	13-0-13
927	Bereshiyt	31	53	13-0-13
1,054	Bereshiyt	36	13	13-0-13
1,081	Bereshiyt	36	40	13-0-13
1,161	Bereshiyt	39	11	13-0-13
1,330	Bereshiyt	44	5	13-0-13
1,375	Bereshiyt	45	16	13-0-13
1,381	Bereshiyt	45	22	13-0-13
1,498	Bereshiyt	49	24	13-0-13
1,515	Bereshiyt	50	8	13-0-13
1,649	Shemot	5	16	13-0-13
1,674	Shemot	6	18	13-0-13
1,831	Shemot	12	14	13-0-13
2,003	Shemot	18	3	13-0-13
2,203	Shemot	25	10	13-0-13
2,254	Shemot	26	21	13-0-13

Vessel	Book	Chp.	Vs.	Form.
2,264	Shemot	26	31	13-0-13
2,308	Shemot	28	17	13-0-13
2,358	Shemot	29	24	13-0-13
2,374	Shemot	29	40	13-0-13
2,438	Shemot	32	2	13-0-13
2,454	Shemot	32	18	13-0-13
2,590	Shemot	36	26	13-0-13
2,642	Shemot	38	11	13-0-13
2,656	Shemot	38	25	13-0-13
2,700	Shemot	39	38	13-0-13
2,972	VaYikra	9	21	13-0-13
3,042	VaYikra	11	47	13-0-13
3,153	VaYikra	14	44	13-0-13
3,181	VaYikra	15	15	13-0-13
3,417	VaYikra	23	17	13-0-13
3,653	BeMidbar	1	51	13-0-13
3,717	BeMidbar	3	27	13-0-13
3,721	BeMidbar	3	31	13-0-13
3,812	BeMidbar	5	22	13-0-13
4,452	BeMidbar	24	8	13-0-13
4,458	BeMidbar	24	14	13-0-13
4,544	BeMidbar	26	57	13-0-13
4,588	BeMidbar	28	13	13-0-13
4,612	BeMidbar	29	6	13-0-13
4,688	BeMidbar	31	26	13-0-13
4,826	BeMidbar	34	12	13-0-13
4,901	Devarim	1	11	13-0-13
4,920	Devarim	1	30	13-0-13

Vessel	Book	Chp.	Vs.	Form.
4,990	Devarim	3	17	13-0-13
5,029	Devarim	4	27	13-0-13
5,152	Devarim	8	20	13-0-13
5,339	Devarim	16	2	13-0-13
5,351	Devarim	16	14	13-0-13
5,422	Devarim	19	21	13-0-13
5,520	Devarim	23	26	13-0-13
5,680	Devarim	29	5	13-0-13
5,695	Devarim	29	20	13-0-13
5,727	Devarim	31	4	13-0-13
5,770	Devarim	32	17	13-0-13
5,788	Devarim	32	35	13-0-13

12. A Sequential Listing of the Vessel Formulation (14-0-14)

Forty-Nine Vessels

Vessel	Book	Chp.	Vs.	Form.
61	Bereshiyt	3	5	14-0-14
204	Bereshiyt	8	20	14-0-14
260	Bereshiyt	10	25	14-0-14
414	Bereshiyt	17	16	14-0-14
454	Bereshiyt	18	29	14-0-14
680	Bereshiyt	25	21	14-0-14
686	Bereshiyt	25	27	14-0-14
786	Bereshiyt	28	12	14-0-14
989	Bereshiyt	34	8	14-0-14
1,084	Bereshiyt	36	43	14-0-14

Vessel	Book	Chp.	Vs.	Form.
1,200	Bereshiyt	41	4	14-0-14
1,462	Bereshiyt	48	10	14-0-14
1,640	Shemot	5	7	14-0-14
1,770	Shemot	9	27	14-0-14
1,835	Shemot	12	18	14-0-14
2,224	Shemot	25	31	14-0-14
2,225	Shemot	25	32	14-0-14
2,288	Shemot	27	18	14-0-14
2,299	Shemot	28	8	14-0-14
2,336	Shemot	29	2	14-0-14
2,357	Shemot	29	23	14-0-14
2,465	Shemot	32	29	14-0-14
2,534	Shemot	35	5	14-0-14
2,620	Shemot	37	18	14-0-14
2,639	Shemot	38	8	14-0-14
2,646	Shemot	38	15	14-0-14
2,913	VaYikra	7	36	14-0-14
2,955	VaYikra	9	4	14-0-14
3,049	VaYikra	12	7	14-0-14
3,131	VaYikra	14	22	14-0-14
3,289	VaYikra	19	10	14-0-14
3,413	VaYikra	23	13	14-0-14
3,441	VaYikra	23	41	14-0-14
3,471	VaYikra	25	4	14-0-14
3,958	BeMidbar	8	21	14-0-14
3,961	BeMidbar	8	24	14-0-14
4,026	BeMidbar	11	4	14-0-14
4,166	BeMidbar	15	15	14-0-14

Vessel	Book	Chp.	Vs.	Form.
4,192	BeMidbar	15	41	14-0-14
4,583	BeMidbar	28	8	14-0-14
4,735	BeMidbar	32	19	14-0-14
4,917	Devarim	1	27	14-0-14
5,014	Devarim	4	12	14-0-14
5,022	Devarim	4	20	14-0-14
5,241	Devarim	12	6	14-0-14
5,277	Devarim	13	11	14-0-14
5,347	Devarim	16	10	14-0-14
5,660	Devarim	28	54	14-0-14
5,684	Devarim	29	9	14-0-14

13. A Sequential Listing of the Vessel Formulation (15-0-15)

Thirty-Two Vessels

Vessel	Book	Chp.	Vs.	Form.
71	Bereshiyt	3	15	15-0-15
153	Bereshiyt	6	15	15-0-15
378	Bereshiyt	15	17	15-0-15
427	Bereshiyt	18	2	15-0-15
1,101	Bereshiyt	37	17	15-0-15
1,222	Bereshiyt	41	26	15-0-15
1,325	Bereshiyt	43	34	15-0-15
1,584	Shemot	3	4	15-0-15
1,828	Shemot	12	11	15-0-15
1,909	Shemot	14	19	15-0-15
2,241	Shemot	26	8	15-0-15

Vessel	Book	Chp.	Vs.	Form.
2,270	Shemot	26	37	15-0-15
2,380	Shemot	29	46	15-0-15
2,579	Shemot	36	15	15-0-15
2,594	Shemot	36	30	15-0-15
2,764	VaYikra	2	4	15-0-15
2,831	VaYikra	5	3	15-0-15
3,040	VaYikra	11	45	15-0-15
3,626	BeMidbar	1	24	15-0-15
3,628	BeMidbar	1	26	15-0-15
3,630	BeMidbar	1	28	15-0-15
3,632	BeMidbar	1	30	15-0-15
3,636	BeMidbar	1	34	15-0-15
3,638	BeMidbar	1	36	15-0-15
3,640	BeMidbar	1	38	15-0-5
3,642	BeMidbar	1	40	15-0-15
3,644	BeMidbar	1	42	15-0-15
4,041	BeMidbar	11	19	15-0-15
4,210	BeMidbar	16	18	15-0-15
4,857	BeMidbar	35	14	15-0-15
5,411	Devarim	19	10	15-0-15
5,731	Devarim	31	8	15-0-15

14. A Sequential Listing of the Vessel Formulation (16-0-16)

Twenty-Eight Vessels

Vessel	Book	Chp.	Vs.	Form.
14	Bereshiyt	1	14	16-0-16

Vessel	Book	Chp.	Vs.	Form.
361	Bereshiyt	14	24	16-0-16
624	Bereshiyt	24	32	16-0-16
682	Bereshiyt	25	23	16-0-16
757	Bereshiyt	27	29	16-0-16
938	Bereshiyt	32	10	16-0-16
1,023	Bereshiyt	35	11	16-0-16
1,151	Bereshiyt	39	1	16-0-16
1,382	Bereshiyt	45	23	16-0-16
1,445	Bereshiyt	47	24	16-0-16
1,499	Bereshiyt	49	5	16-0-16
1,889	Shemot	13	21	16-0-16
1,915	Shemot	14	25	16-0-16
2,237	Shemot	26	4	16-0-16
2,243	Shemot	26	10	16-0-16
2,281	Shemot	27	11	16-0-16
2,440	Shemot	32	4	16-0-16
2,575	Shemot	36	11	16-0-16
2,648	Shemot	38	17	16-0-16
3,464	VaYikra	24	20	16-0-16
3,483	VaYikra	25	16	16-0-16
3,512	VaYikra	25	45	16-0-16
3,584	VaYikra	27	16	16-0-16
4,055	BeMidbar	11	33	16-0-16
4,587	BeMidbar	28	12	16-0-16
4,932	Devarim	1	42	16-0-16
5,069	Devarim	5	18	16-0-16
5,807	Devarim	33	2	16-0-16

15. *A Sequential Listing of the Vessel Formulation (17-0-17)*

Twenty-One Vessels

Vessel	Book	Chp.	Vs.	Form.
103	Bereshiyt	4	23	17-0-17
488	Bereshiyt	19	30	17-0-17
1,144	Bereshiyt	38	24	17-0-17
1,333	Bereshiyt	44	8	17-0-17
1,663	Shemot	6	7	17-0-17
1,720	Shemot	8	5	17-0-17
2,286	Shemot	27	16	17-0-17
2,306	Shemot	28	15	17-0-17
2,361	Shemot	29	27	17-0-17
2,416	Shemot	30	36	17-0-17
2,658	Shemot	38	27	17-0-17
3,514	VaYikra	25	47	17-0-17
3,535	VaYikra	26	13	17-0-17
3,634	BeMidbar	1	32	17-0-17
4,620	BeMidbar	29	14	17-0-17
4,738	BeMidbar	32	22	17-0-17
5,016	Devarim	4	14	17-0-17
5,082	Devarim	6	1	17-0-17
5,171	Devarim	9	19	17-0-17
5,415	Devarim	19	14	17-0-17
5,617	Devarim	28	11	17-0-17

16. A Sequential Listing of the Vessel Formulation (18-0-18)

Fifteen Vessels

Vessel	Book	Chp.	Vs.	Form.
1,223	Bereshiyt	41	27	18-0-18
1,964	Shemot	16	16	18-0-18
2,258	Shemot	26	25	18-0-18
3,475	VaYikra	25	8	18-0-18
4,030	BeMidbar	11	8	18-0-18
4,209	BeMidbar	16	17	18-0-18
4,343	BeMidbar	21	5	18-0-18
4,351	BeMidbar	21	13	18-0-18
4,589	BeMidbar	28	14	18-0-18
5,007	Devarim	4	5	18-0-18
5,247	Devarim	12	12	18-0-18
5,631	Devarim	28	25	18-0-18
5,637	Devarim	28	31	18-0-18
5,792	Devarim	32	39	18-0-18
5,838	Devarim	34	4	18-0-18

17. A Sequential Listing of the Vessel Formulation (19-0-19)

Three Vessels

Vessel	Book	Chp.	Vs.	Form.
1,178	Bereshiyt	40	5	19-0-19
3,841	BeMidbar	6	20	19-0-19
4,681	BeMidbar	31	19	19-0-19

18. A Sequential Listing of the Vessel Formulation (20-0-20)

Six Vessels

Vessel	Book	Chp.	Vs.	Form.
787	Bereshiyt	28	13	20-0-20
1,093	Bereshiyt	37	9	20-0-20
1,164	Bereshiyt	39	14	20-0-20
3,996	BeMidbar	10	10	20-0-20
5,048	Devarim	4	46	20-0-20
5,084	Devarim	6	3	20-0-20

19. A Sequential Listing of the Vessel Formulation (21-0-21)

Two Vessels

Vessel	Book	Chp.	Vs.	Form.
2,649	Shemot	38	18	21-0-21
5,539	Devarim	24	19	21-0-21

20. A Sequential Listing of the Vessel Formulation (25-0-25)

One Vessel

Vessel	Book	Chp.	Vs.	Form.
5,348	Devarim	16	11	25-0-25

About the Author

Phillip's father returned from the Great War in the winter of 1945, and nine months later, Phillip was born in North Wildwood, New Jersey. He was born into a secular Christian family and was baptized as an infant in the Methodist church.

He graduated from Lower Cape May Regional High School (1964) and began his apprenticeship in the carpentry trade. Following his apprenticeship, he became a residential building contractor. Having experienced a life-changing encounter with the Creator, he set his course to learn the ways of the Creator. He began his Biblical studies at Asbury College in 1975 and eventually received his BA in Bible from Oral Roberts University in 1987. He later received a Virginia teacher's certification from Norfolk State University and taught in elementary school for seven years.

It was during his studies at ORU that he realized that the traditional Christian faith was incompatible with his feelings, and his desire to study Hebrew and Torah began to consume him. He investigated the Hebrew roots movement, the messianic Jewish movement, and the Noahide movement, and soon realized their shortcomings when compared to the standards of the Torah. Some are satisfied with shades of grey, but not him. He considered converting to Judaism, but even that failed to satisfy his inner yearnings. He set his face to the Torah, solely to the Torah, and the marvelous truths that are presented here and in his other studies have taken his relationship with his Father far beyond what he ever could have dreamed. Blessed be *HaShem*, my Father, my Master, and my God.

Throughout his entire working life, he continued his connection with the building trades, working his way through college, even while teaching. The whole of his vocational skills has prepared him for the task at hand, understanding and illustrating the numerical structure of the Torah.

Currently, Phillip is a Torah observant gentile with no religious institutional connections.

CPSIA information can be obtained
at www.ICGtesting.com
Printed in the USA
LVHW070935180321
681657LV00035B/899